Transparency

Poetic Confessions of a Transparent Gem, Vol. 1

Compiled by Natima Sheree

A Transparent Gem Inc Publication

Published by: Transparent Gem Inc.

ISBN: 9798386505134

Printed in the United States of America

First Edition

Contents

Prologue...1

Hidden Gems...2

The Power of Air 16

X Man 18

Quiet Storm 20

Queen.. 42

Ripples.. 44

The Fall of Sam.. 46

Lost 53

Grounded.. 54

Features 56

The Purpose Of An Unplanned Pregnancy 58

Black Excellence 65

Forged By Fire.. 66

Overcoming Hurt 68

Resistance 92

Parental Remorse 93

All Life...112

Now I See Me...Now You Don't....................................114

Soul Remission...131

Prologue

Patricia Robinson

Learning to master your best potential is the essence of leaning into all of your prior experiences. Leaning in will give you a purview of the experiences including challenges, successes, personal evolving, happiness, disappointments from people, confidence, fear, and humility.

Making sure to understand the external environment including the ever-evolving competitive landscape is essential. However, true success is measured directly in how you hold yourself fully accountable for your personal growth. I have not always been recognized for my value and contributions in spaces where I should have been. However, I did not give up on myself, I put that fault where it belonged- to those who chose to "not see me". I didn't understand it back then but have recognized that my light exposed dark spaces over the years. It made people uncomfortable.

Ultimately, I had to decide if I was going to adjust my light or shine the way I was designed to. I chose myself.

Do not sacrifice who you know you can be to make others comfortable. Position yourself so people must get used to your full existence.

You deserve to be seen and experienced in all your greatness.

Hidden Gems

Written in The Dark

Natima Sheree

Transmute Pain into Light

"Even stars need darkness to shine." – Unknown

Dear Gem,

I began writing this chapter and compiling this anthology during one of the darkest periods of my life. I had been in a perpetual season of loss and lack and was feeling the pressure in an intense and suffocating way. Although I cannot recall exactly when, I was certain that I had lost my light at some point in the past decade or so. It could have been when I lost my younger sister in 2015 or when I lost my home to a flood and was forced to live in a hotel with my two small children in 2017. Maybe it happened when I filed for bankruptcy following my divorce in 2011, or when I heard the terrifying and life-threatening words, "cervical cancer" in 2012. Perhaps it was in 2014 after suffering from job loss during the infamous government shutdown; when I struggled to provide for my daughter and was forced to swallow my pride, disregarding my advanced academic training and professional experience to take a minimum-wage job at Target. My innate light could have burned out when I was six months pregnant with my youngest daughter and her father initiated his incessant leave of absence in 2016. Or it could have been a result of small and consistent infractions and offenses that I've endured; some self-imposed

2

and others caused by people I loved, trusted, and cared for. Whichever life event, tragedy, or trauma, I am confident at some point I had lost my light. I had lost my will to live.

There is nothing more devastating than forgetting who you are. To no longer see value in yourself or realize your own significance. Hearing others tell me how blessed, talented, and gifted I was when everything around me had been slowly falling apart was frustrating. I cringed when people would attempt to tell me, how much God loved me when I felt punished and abandoned by him.

Have you ever felt so empty, alone, and broken that all you could do was cry? Have you ever cried so hard and for so long that the sound of your own tears and agony became too much, so you cover your own mouth trying to smother the sound of your cry? Well, I have.

There was a time when tears were my only form of communication. My tears had become my prayers, outcry, protest, and response to life.

I would spend my days in character, performing for those who regarded me as strong, independent, and unbothered. And would cry myself to sleep at night. Trauma, tragedy, challenges, and hardship had become a revolving and reoccurring cycle and season of life for me. There were intervals of happiness, but it seemed that none of the joyous times outlasted or outweighed the tough times. At least not from my perspective.

There was a cadence of disappointment and struggle. Everything seemed so difficult and so hard. Life had become so overwhelming that I felt sick. I was battling dis·ease (disease). Eventually, my physical appearance embodied my internal disorder. I was tired all the time, irritable, angry, upset, and discontented. I was popping Tylenol and Motrin-like M&Ms to manage the migraines and tension headaches. I was complaining and crying daily. My light had surely gone out. I was completely burnt out. I was exhausted. I had been consumed by emotional, spiritual, mental, and energetic darkness.

Now I wish I could tell you that a miraculous experience finally drew me out of this dark place, but that is not my testimony. There was no "major move of God" that brought me to the other side. There was no rescue, deliverance, or breakthrough. I made a simple decision. Instead of resisting the darkness, I began to accept it. Acceptance helped me to see myself, my circumstances, and my life experiences in dark places so differently. This way of thinking was transitional and transformational and helped me to reconsider my experiences. I never lost my light; I was simply being challenged to shine brighter.

The introspective work, referred to as "shadow work" that this protracted season prompted, taught me that shadow is evidence of light in dark places. I was the light all along. I want to encourage you, if this is a familiar space or similar season that you are experiencing, don't be consumed by the darkness, be inspired by it. Darkness provides an opportunity for you to shine. Learning to transmute my pain into light was the most freeing and empowering transition of my life.

Treasure is hidden in dark places, and I believe God has a purpose for everything we go through.

Life is a journey, and we will all experience the season of night. The night season is also referred to as dark periods of life that are low visibility and bleak, low vibrational, lonely, and still. Seasons that you feel hopeless, obscure, and overwhelming internal warfare. This is not uncommon, and you are not being punished. You have the resilience, the fortitude, and the power to push through. You are enough. Your light is enough.

Instead of resisting the darkness, look for the purpose, the hidden treasure, the opportunity. Be inspired by this season of transition to let things go, let old parts of you die, and embrace the light that is in front of you. The light that is in you. The light that is you. No matter how dark it gets at night, we know the sun will always come up and shine. The darkness taught me to appreciate the light. My light.

Made of Magic

"Just because we're magic, doesn't mean we're not real." – Jesse Williams

In the Diamond Writers' first anthology, I contributed a chapter entitled "Pretty Strong." I remember drafting the chapter and writing from such a transparent yet proud space. I wore strength like a badge of honor. I robed myself in strength as if being strong was a privilege, accolade, or accomplishment. Little did I know or realize I was setting myself up for failure. I was confusing strength with perfection. I mistook strength for impassiveness and used strength as a mask for my disappointment and pain. I had adopted the strong black woman trope, so to speak.

It wasn't until my S.A.V.A.G.E healing journey that I learned just how damaging and self-destructive a consistent posture of strength can be. I viewed weakness and frailty as failure and associated strength with perfectionism; a trait I didn't come to know as unhealthy until now.

Society consistently tells black and brown women that above all else, be strong. Society depicts BIPOC women as an endless source of resilience, strength, tenacity, and fortitude. Black women have been told to survive and even thrive without love, support, help, appreciation, or rest. We honor and celebrate the black single mother who can provide for her family, pursue higher education, build a career, serve her community, and chase her dreams even if it costs her physical or mental health. Subliminal messages in media influence women to "secure the bag," and to relentlessly chase success. To prioritize success and not self. To sacrifice everything for prominence and fame.

I look at all the successful women in media, in politics, in corporate America, in Hollywood and ask myself "but are they happy? Are they healthy? Are they fulfilled?" Sure, we have degrees, hold positions of power, influence multitudes in media, and shatter glass ceilings in business, leading movements and spearheading global initiatives and organizations of change; but are we really happy? Do we lose ourselves in the process? Have we traded the true essence of womanhood for the favor of feminism?

Now I can't and won't attempt to speak for all black and brown women, I can and will only speak for myself. And my answer is NO! No, I was not happy! I was not fulfilled. I was not healthy. I was exhausted. I had material rewards, professional credentials, and accomplishments but lacked love, true friendship, and genuine connection with others. I had all the tangible things I wanted but had none of the transcendent things my soul craved and my spirit desired. I was a hollow force. I had the power to make things happen and move things forward in my life, but I, myself, was completely empty and void of significance. The illusion of strength had clouded my vision.

Like so many women, I believed I had to choose. That I couldn't have a successful career and a healthy love life. That I couldn't have genuine friendships and be a boss chick. I was convinced that my life only had room for one precedence and everything else would be a hindrance or distraction.

Starting my healing journey and focusing on my innate worth, I have a completely different set of goals and desires. I am no longer hinging my magic and power on the material things I possess, the titles or hats I wear, or the accomplishments and accolades I achieve; but rather the impact I have on others. The love and appreciation I receive and the way I make others feel. I am no longer concerned with how many followers I have but rather how many people I can successfully lead. I am focused on making others feel heard, seen, and appreciated. I am intentional in redirecting my energy investment. Pursuing what makes me happy and empowering meaningful connections. I am letting go of the labels, abandoning grind culture, and surrendering perfectionism. I am spending more time doing what I love, doing what makes me smile and brings me joy. I am not stingy with my energy, as the trending low vibrational memes would try to influence, but rather sharing the best parts of my personality and temperament with others, in hopes that my positive vibe would ignite something in them subliminally encouraging them to do the same. I am intentionally kind, philanthropic, and jovial.

I am still strong but not for the same reasons or in the same ways I valued before. Now, I am strong enough to be vulnerable, strong enough to be soft, and strong enough to say sorry or to ask for help. I am strong enough to admit when I don't feel strong.

Gem, I want you to know that your magic is innate, and your strength is but one small part of it. The depth of who you are and what fashioned your black girl magic cannot be defined or contained. There is no label, title, or position in life that can adequately reflect your worth, value, and sheer greatness.

No matter what season you find yourself in, go inward and tap into all your magic. Not just the parts that the world celebrates, but the parts of you that make you unapologetically unique... and that my friend takes strength.

Energy & Love

"Love is infectious and the greatest healing energy." – Sai Baba

I was listening to a sermon by Pastor Ben Stuart, and he said, "the magnitude of your healing must match the magnitude of your wound..." (paraphrased). I replayed this in my mind several times as I began to reflect on the last year of my life when I had been on an intentional healing journey. I thought about my heartbreak recovery, emotional healing, and self-forgiveness, and asked myself, "have my healing efforts matched or coincided with the magnitude of my wounds?" In my head, I heard a loud and clear "NO!"

In that moment of self-reflection, I admitted that I had been consumed by the rituals, habits, and routines of the healing process but hadn't tapped into the source and force of healing, which is love. I had been dedicated for almost a year to my healing journey but still lacked love. I thought by choosing to heal I was showing myself love, which in many ways I was, however, I learned that when attempting to heal trauma, self-love is not enough. You will need the love of family, friends, a spouse, children, etc. to completely heal your emotional wounds.

8

I was caught up in "healing adjacent" which is learning to recover and survive trauma without actually healing from it. This is also referred to as "coping with trauma." What recovery, survival, and coping lack that true and holistic healing has, is LOVE. The years of pain, disappointment, hurt, and heartache I wanted to heal required the most powerful remedy, medicine, treatment, and cure, which I will emphasize, is love.

Like many, I had taken cues from social media and religion and convinced myself that isolation was the way to heal; that being alone and shutting people out was the appropriate way to mend all that had been broken in me. But I could not have been more wrong. I needed people; their support, their love, their energy, and their presence to heal. I can admit that I could probably be so much further in my healing journey had a realized this sooner and invited people in.

So, Gem, allow me to share with you a few of the steps I'm taking to prioritize love as the driving force in my healing journey.

Self-Love

Love heals from the inside out. It starts with you, then flows to others, and allows you to receive from others. Everything in our lives flows out from within us. Our thoughts, intentions, and feelings, all flow from within us. Therefore, love must be within us to flow from us. You must become immersed in love and in loving/positive things. Use affirmations, mantras, stories, poetry, music, etc. to nurture and influence loving thoughts. Make the choice to become a more loving person. Don't base this on others, don't create a contingency, but decide to be a loving person for yourself. Don't withhold love waiting on others to reciprocate or extend it first. Give love and show love freely, this action will attract and draw authentic love toward you, both romantic and platonic.

Love yourself, by taking care of yourself, mentally, emotionally, spiritually, energetically, and physically. Set boundaries for yourself. Speak kind words to yourself and be patient with your growth and healing.

Connection

Social and intimate connections help us heal and improve physical, mental and emotional well-being. It is proven that social and romantic connection lowers anxiety, and depression and enhances self-esteem. Forming greater social connections will remove feelings of loneliness and abandonment and help us to feel supported and cared for. Spending time with loved ones while healing will take your mind off your trauma and allow you to focus your energy on positivity and meaningful engagement.

Validation

I read in an article years ago that said "if you don't validate your own internal experience, then you undermine your self-worth." This statement became real to me during my healing journey because I became well acquainted with the benefits of self-validation as a form of love. Self-validation is not the same as self-love but is just as important to your healing. When healing, validating yourself sends the message that "my feelings and emotions matter. My healing is a priority and is important to me." Not only does validation reflect this behavior back to you but you project this out to others as well, allowing them to support you in your journey.

I want to leave you with this gem, "love's ability to heal is not magical, instantaneous, or superficial; love is not merely a feeling but an energetic force that can create, change and save lives. Love is a healer."

Growth Hurts

"We can't become what we need to be by remaining what we are."
– Oprah Winfrey

I read a meme that said, "real growth is when you are tired of your own shit." And I felt that because I remember getting to this point... when I finally grew tired of the inner me being my greatest enemy. I was tired of feeling defeated by my own negative thoughts and overwhelmed by fear and doubt. I was tired of existing and not living because of my unhealed trauma and brokenness.

I was finally fed up enough to initiate genuine healing, growth, and change. I had a mirror-facing moment and intently examined myself.

Here are a few things I did to change my mind, heart condition, and habits to cultivate growth and peace:

1. Stop blaming others for where you are, what you've been through, and how you feel. This is not to say others haven't attributed or contributed to your hurt, stagnancy, or stalled life but misplaced blame or misdirected accountability will not help you to deal with yourself. Accept that every decision you've made are the decisions YOU made, regardless of external influences. Own it and make the decision to do better and better. Your growth depends on this first step.

2. Stop looking to or waiting for others to save you. You are responsible for your healing, and happiness. There is not one person or connection that will do the work for you. The temporary happiness others may bring or prompt you to feel cannot compare to the permanent joy and peace that working on yourself will furnish.

3. See yourself outside yourself. In other words, get out of your head and out your feelings. View yourself in a non-judgmental but honest and holistic way. When you recognize things about your personality, mindset, temperament, energy, and vibe that you don't like, or you can admit maybe repelling others, get to work on changing them. Develop new habits and attitudes that will foster change and attract positivity.

Uncensored

"I'm not afraid of my truth anymore, and I will not omit pieces of myself to make you more comfortable." – Alex Elle

To "live your truth" can mean a lot of things depending on whom you're talking to. However, since you're reading my chapter, I'm going to tell you what "living your truth" means to me.

For me, living your truth means to live as your most authentic self, to do things that bring you joy and make you happy; to be true to yourself, and to own your mistakes but not allow them to define you. To be honest with yourself and with others.

Despite our best efforts to live life on our own terms, it's human nature to be influenced by our environment, media, friends, and family. And as much as we'd love to believe we live life our way, many of us live and make decisions based on social and peer validation and acceptance. We are afraid to expose the world to whom we really are out of fear that we will be rejected or mocked.

In the same way, our experiences dictate how free, and liberated we live or how limited and constricted we live. In my adolescent years, I was unapologetically myself. I was sure of myself, excited about life, and untainted by fear, stigmas, stereotypes, and the burden of others' opinions. However, the older I got, the more I lived, and the more I interacted with others, the less confident I felt, the more inferior I felt, and the more I tried to live for others' approval.

I was slowly shrinking, diluting who I was and conforming to what others desired and wanted from me.

Every time I was vocal and disagreed with someone, I was called difficult. Every time I stood in my power and exercised my authority, I was called masculine. And every time I set and enforced boundaries, I was called rigid and inflexible. These labels and markers caused me to question myself, to conform and adapt to the image of me I thought others expected and wanted.

Eventually, I began suffering from an identity crisis. I was frustrated, I felt stuck and lacked progression. I was extremely uncomfortable with my life. All my decisions were based on what I thought others would say or think, not realizing then that I would be the only one living with the consequences of my decisions, regardless of their input or influence.

At some point, maturity and peace redirected my outlook and shaped a new perspective. I was done living for the approval and acceptance of others. It was clear that no matter what I did to appease people, I would never win their approval, endorsement, or validation.

Truth is that most people aren't even happy with themselves. Their consistent judgment, ridicule, and unsolicited opinion of you and your life are how they cope and escape the harsh reality and the unhappiness of their own.

One of the greatest gifts I awarded myself during my healing journey was a boundless and excellent life. I gave myself permission to do any and everything I wanted. I am chasing dreams that seem unrealistic, I am traveling to places and experiencing things that I was told a girl from Queens never would. I'm living a limitless, unapologetic, and uncensored life and I encourage you to do the same! Go to places you didn't think you could. Try new things. Take fashion risks. Pursue new opportunities. Support things you love. Do things that excite you. Post and share things that interest you. Be who you are, in every way!

Born. Becoming. Being

"You are the one that possesses the keys to your being. You carry the passport to your happiness." – Diane Von Furstenberg

Although brief, I hope the transparency and honesty in my chapter have provided you with both insight and inspiration. I hope that something I've shared or said will ignite a fire in you and prompt you to pursue a similar journey of your own. I hope that my hidden gems will be a source of light revealing what lies deep within you and that God gives you the courage to uncover the pain points that may be keeping you from living a fulfilled and whole life.

This past year has been one of the hardest yet most amazing years of my life. I lost so much but gained even more in rediscovering myself. I had to unlearn some things and relearn some things. I had to forfeit some things and adopt some things. I had to abandon some things and attract some things. And all of it was for my good.

I want to leave you with a few best practices that are helping me as I become the best version of myself.

1. Always keep learning – try to learn something new from whatever you do. Try to find the positive in all things and learn from what you experience!

2. Make yourself better – don't waste time trying to be like others; spend your time making yourself better.

3. Observe deeply – Watch what is going on around you. Pay attention to your interactions, energy exchanges, etc. Be mindful of where you are investing your time and energy.

4. Avoid time-wasting habits – time is a precious and priceless gift. Don't waste it scrolling, comparing yourself to others, or dwelling on what you lack or don't yet have.

No matter what you desire in life, I can guarantee you will not receive it until the healed version of you emerges. There are things that you are waiting for, that are waiting on you. Waiting on you to heal, grow, mature, and change. There are opportunities that won't come to this version of you. Only the healed you will be strong enough to hold all that is for you. So do the work because I can promise you that everything you desire, desires you!

The Power of Air

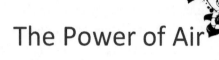

Fionix

Gem for this meditation, I ask, if possible, for you to go outside or sit near an open window. Sit comfortably on the floor of the space you are in. Close your eyes and drop your head. Gently place your open hands upon your chest. This is your heart space. Allow your body to function by design. This means releasing control for a moment and letting go. I know that may be frightening but we must trust the process. We must learn to trust ourselves.

I remind you that YOU do not need to tell your blood to flow or your lungs to breathe. That is because this is what they are meant to do. Feel this rise and fall of your chest. Your inhales and exhales should be rhythmic. If not, are you anxious? Are you tense? What are you thinking about? Gem, it is time for you to relax. It is time to steady yourself.

The element of air is often overlooked. We do not think much about air because we cannot see it. We cannot touch it. It is not tangible. Yet the power of air is all around us. We can hear it rustle in the leaves of a tree. We can see the blades of a windmill spin. And, on a blustery day, we can feel its resistance against our bodies, pushing and pulling us in different directions. Therefore, we must recognize the power of air.

Let's take this moment now to be one with the air we take into our bodies. Slowly inhale for a count of four. Sit with that breath for a count of four. Slowly exhale for a count of four. Sit with the release for a count of four. Try not to hold your breath. Use all the counts to fully inflate your lungs and then completely empty them. Repeat those three more times. This technique is called box breathing. It is used to distract a busy mind. It will calm your nervous system and relieve you of stress.

As you were breathing, did you begin to sway? Did the curve of your spine become more pronounced? Did you become one with the power of air?

Continue to breathe gem. Think of the balance that must exist on this planet for us all to survive. We inhale into our body wonderful oxygen. That oxygen nourishes our blood, our tissue, and our organs. Then we release into the atmosphere carbon dioxide which the plants and trees use for their growth and survival. In turn, they give us back more oxygen.

WOW!! ISN'T THAT AMAZING!! You are amazing. Your breath contributes to the sustainability of this planet.

In order for the planet to be plentiful, there must be balance, and that balance starts simply with you remembering that it is okay for you to just breathe.

X Man

Natima Sheree

When he speaks, it's as if time has been interrupted by the flow of his energetic expression and rhetoric.

I find myself falling deeper into presence of mind when I am enveloped in the security of his masculinity.

He caresses the inmost parts of me without physical touch and massages my heart once mishandled and bruised by past lovers.

Handsome fails to adequately define his makeup and build.

His ebony skin lays oh so perfectly against his God fashioned physic complimentary of his innate glow.

I get lost in him and have no desire to escape.

I crave his energy and the peace it offers.

I am addicted to the scent of his aura and captivated by the transparency of his manhood.

He penetrates me with promises of authentic connection, and I become overwhelmed by the fear of its loss.

I see him, all of him. His deep thoughts he conceals behind a veneer of a casual calm.

I can see his desire for affection and sincere love buried by an egoic timidity.

I recognize the man he is and is becoming and celebrate his maturing greatness.

I am infatuated with his kindness and gentleness. Obsessed with his affection and embrace.

I desire to be his safe space. His peace. His lover. His best friend. I want to be his One.

Quiet Storm

Lady J A

Dear Gem...for years you quietly struggled with the emotions of not fully understanding the dynamics of your father's inconsistent presence. The consequence seemingly falls on your young shoulders creating hurt that will appear to be unfair, unwarranted, and unintelligible. The promises are broken and lack follow-through, leaving you waiting by the door hoping this time will be different. It will feel as if there is no end to the letdowns, traumas, and horrors. The cyclone begins with the inability of the man who should have loved you first to be accountable, available, and present. In an effort to protect yourself from future hurt you become closed off to people who show any indication of illusive behavior. The storms appear to come consecutively, perhaps never-ending but only changing feeder bands and intensity. Nothing about this journey will be easy; abandonment, neglect, and betrayal will be the resonating theme. The kind of storm when the thunder rubbles your body trembles with fear at the very sound. This storm is going to put you through a wave of emotions, you will surmount and see a radiance that even you did not imagine possible. In fact, it will show you the strength that lies within you. This strength will not only carry you through this season, but it will also propel you into a life that you never imagined possible. Realizing what appears to be the worst circumstances ends up being your blessing. This storm will change course during this journey to self, feeling no one even realizes the pain battled within.

August 2001, you are preparing to return to school for your sophomore year of college. Standing in the middle aisle of your church sanctuary facing a white casket with flowers on either side. As you slowly walk closer the image inside becomes visible, Mommy? As you wake from a nap to the touch of your mother's hand gently rubbing the side of your face, as she so often did, there is a tear. She asked, "What is the matter, did you have a bad dream?" Reluctantly you answer, "Yes". Yet could not share the details of what you saw, somehow, she knows and asks. "Was it about me?" As you shake your head Yes, she looks right down into your eyes and says, "I will be ok". Reluctantly you return to school and by the third week, mommy gets admitted into the hospital with coumadin toxicity. Somehow her physical condition gets worse, she goes from getting up to use the bathroom, to using a commode, to a bedpan, then to diapers. Her body appears to be succumbing to illness, yet to be identified, to the point where she can barely wipe her mouth. After a month in the hospital, she was discharged to a rehabilitation facility. Two weeks later the phone rings at around 1:00 AM, your brother is calling, Mommy has been admitted into the ICU with respiratory failure and they don't think she will make it. Unable to think clearly, your roommate offers to drive you to the hospital in the middle of the night, over an hour and a half away. Without a second thought, you pack up and take what appears to be the longest ride of your life. So many thoughts of what will be once you arrive. "Will she be responsive?" "Am I too late to say goodbye?" "What will I do if she does not pull through?"

Walking into the ICU, nothing can prepare you for what you will see. Tubes everywhere and her unresponsive body is swollen from the fluids beyond recognition. This image is one that won't go away, it will replay in your mind haunting your thoughts and occupying memories for years to come. God will give you a few more months after this with her, she will be alert but unable to speak because of the tracheotomy. School gets put on the back burner, to the point where you will not show up for final exams. Your focus is off, and worry runs deep and even though you know she wants you at school, you cannot bear to leave her side. While your professors understand, your academics suffer but that is the least of your concerns. Mid-October, your Uncle Butch dies, one of the few men who made a point to make you feel special. To genuinely love and care about your well-being, even in the midst of his own struggles. Could not bear to tell Mommy, but somehow the news finds her anyway. She is so weak; she could barely get her tears to flow. What can you say at this moment, it was a major loss to the family. To make matters worse she seems to be declining more each day. Early November you come home to a padlocked door with a letter from the sheriff, NOTICE OF EVICTION. Mommy cannot know, it will only worry her and negatively impact her recovery. Family and friends come together to secure the funds for a storage unit, and everything gets moved, but it does not seem Mommy is getting strong enough to be weaned off the respirator. "Where will she go once discharged?" In your mind, you have quit school and decided to find full-time work to help with her care.

Until the night of December 22nd…your god sister is singing as mommy does her little shake in the bed, watching football with your brother, seems she is showing improvement! But you notice fluid weeping from her arm and her neck swelling around the band holding the trach in place. Everything in you did not want to leave her that night but she made you go. Before leaving you tell her that everyone is praying for her and remember she is not alone. She looks at you and says, "No, you remember you are not alone. Promise me you will not quit school". Of course, you agree to the promise, leaving saying "I love you" to each other. The next day, Sunday, December 23, arriving at the hospital after church but she is no longer alert or even responding to you, it is almost as if only the machine is keeping her alive. Her lips look a pasty white, her body is inert and the sounds of the respirator seem to reverberate off of each wall. The doctor calls and informs her that cancer has returned to her liver, and they need to start chemotherapy right away. You declined treatment because you knew that this would not help or improve her condition. Walking back to the room, your mind is racing, nothing is making sense. Lying in the bed with your mom one last time, you whisper in her ear, "Mommy, it is ok to let go, I will be ok. I don't want you to suffer anymore." A few moments later vitals start to drop, you are escorted to the "quiet room", overhead you can hear code blue called. 5:41 pm The doctor walks in the room and informs you, Mommy didn't make it. Walking back to the room everything feels still and quiet, almost as if you alone are walking through a tunnel. There is such calm and peace in the room that you almost feel comforted. Mommy looks the best you have seen her in years, the tears could not even form, numb to the notion that your every day will be changed forever. Her face once again had color, the expression on her face was one of relief and contentment. I now spend her favorite holiday, Christmas, planning her funeral and burial. When you call to notify your father of her passing words are exchanged and he hangs up on you. The trigger was he asked for you to be strong for him, you let him know you will for your mother because that is what she taught you. After all the years of disappointments, letdowns, and total disregard for your heart this situation was no different. It left you empty confirming that all you really had was, to figure out what was next and how you would get through this storm that is your new reality. Nothing about this felt real, this only fed the cyclone of emotions created by his indifference to my heart.

It was decided to have the wake and funeral the same day, with the holidays here it was best to make sure she was laid to rest before the New Year came in. Ironically, walking into that church was exactly as you dreamed, a white casket with flowers on each side. It felt as though God was preparing you, nothing could brace you for what was to come. It is going to get worse before it gets better. Gem, it is now the day of, and he shows up. When you see him, you try to walk the other way without him noticing, unfortunately, it won't work. He calls out to you and even in your attempt not to hear him, he follows you. You meet in a pew, it starts off well, but it only lasts for a moment. He tells you he is proud of you and how well you did with Mommy's arrangements. Then he says, "There is Father's Day and I do have a birthday." You try to take the high road and tell him, "I cannot do this right now, let's talk later." But he will insist, and it allows you to release all the thoughts you have kept festering inside for years. "Father's Day and a birthday? I have had a birthday for 20 years and cannot remember one time you called, sent a card, or acknowledged me in some way. You only remember my name because I am named after your mother." The best part is when he says, "I have told you about your mouth." At this point you just let it go, "How could you tell me anything about myself when I go years without a phone call, and when it does happen it is because I called you? My mother was in the hospital for 3 months and you never checked on her or me. You didn't know if I had food to eat or a place to lay my head. But you never cared to know anything about me, have you?" Gem, it gets so heated that people are now separating the two of you and he leaves. This is your father, the man that should be protecting and comforting you at this moment. It was so bad you walked up to Mommy's casket apologizing and asking her forgiveness.

Returning to school that January will be surreal, your whole life has changed and literally everything is different. The new friends you made will be your biggest support, mainly because you have closed yourself off to the idea that anyone will care like your mom did. Your godparents will do all they can to support given they live in a different state. Still reeling from all that changed in the 3 months prior you are numb to reality. Because of the lack of attention to your studies the previous semester you now must do an extra year and really dive in to reclaim your academic status. Life happens before you thought you were ready, getting up every day, feeling empty operating solely on the promise you made to her, that is what will keep you going.

Mid-February you receive a message from financial aid saying you must make arrangements to pay the 17,000-dollar balance or you will have to move out of the dorm. Just when the thunder rumbling seemed to be inaudible, here we are. Admittedly you are not going to know what to do, your friends are going to tell you not to give up, but you are going to feel you have no other option. You have never been one to fold so you go to financial aid to see what could be done. Once there they confirm what the message said and told you to come back at the end of the week to make sure there are no changes. At this point, you begin packing and trying to figure out where you can stay until this is figured out. As recommended you return that Friday for an update. There is someone different at the counter and you can feel your pulse in every extremity. If there is no change, you have nowhere to go, there is no other plan. "Danielle, you have a credit of $3,223.67", that is a number you won't soon forget. "A credit? Are you sure that is my account? Had a balance of $17,000." Because of your mother's passing, your status changed from dependent to independent which increases the range of available aid from grants, TAP, and SEOG. After understanding how this happened you will ask to speak with the person who approved these changes. Only seeing the initials, she goes to look for the person J.A.B., and she comes back a little confused. Saying, "There is no one in this office with those initials". This could be by chance, but Mommy's name was Judith Ann Bishop. She said you would not be alone, and this will be one of many sweet reminders. Gem, this is life-changing... Finally, it feels like the bone-shaking thunderstorm is passing over!

April of 2002, you meet someone, and this relationship is going to take you on so many waves of emotions. Yes, I know we don't do nonsense, we are the queen of the pack-a-bag tribe. Soft translation, we go at the first sight of some mess! But this is going to teach you the power of forgiveness and the value of releasing the idea that every man is like your father. Most young girls look for this without realizing it, but you made it your purpose to identify any characteristic that was a reminder of him and immediately abort! This guy is going to love you to your core and see your value before you accept it for yourself. Of course, we don't let on that we are broken, because well we just don't have the time to fall apart. Instead, we have up a wall that scared off many but only took one to see through.

It is the annual dance show, and while waiting for your act to be called up you see Shawn cut the corner down the hall. He had on a red fitted cap, white tee (you know the ones down to the mid-thigh) red sweatpants, and of course the matching red and white uptowns. Oh, but don't forget the diamond-incrusted chain with the cross. Nothing about this felt religious but it was a nice touch. He was everything you said you would not date, but something about him made me take notice. The back story is he showed interest in freshman year and you did not return his calls. Since he was a junior at the time, it was clear he was interested in something you were not giving. Here we are a year later, and he looks different in your eyes or maybe it is your awareness. Your friend sees your reaction and says, "Go say hi". After giving her the look of Are you out of your mind, you find yourself walking down the hall hoping he takes notice? The whole time you are saying to yourself, "Girl what are you doing...this is going to give groupie vibes". Walking past you exchange greetings, and you keep walking but have no destination because you are supposed to be on the other side. Should have known something was off here, got me doing things that make no sense! Your paths will cross again at the library, now you went a year on the same campus and never saw each other, but now two encounters within a week. He asked you out to a movie and that was the start of your friendship. There was no pressure, no awkwardness, no creep vibes; just good energy. Established a meeting spot at the steps of the "campus green" and connected over burgers from the diner. This went on until his graduation in May.

It felt natural and real, someone who genuinely took an interest in you as a person. But (all knew it was coming), telling yourself not to allow the heart to get too invested in this. Anything you decide to do, make sure you are good with having to walk away with no regret. What you will realize later is this came from a place of not feeling worthy of a man spending time on you. Believing that a man will genuinely express interest in you without wanting something in return was hard to accept. Simply because your father did not, he never showed you how a man should treat you. Let's face it, if your father would not take the time with you, why would a man you barely know? The only thing he accomplished was teaching you how rejection, disinterest, and heartache felt. So, we spend a lot of time half communicating because why invest too much time and emotion in someone who is bound to let you down?

Thunder has stopped and the rumbles no longer take over my thoughts. He asked you to his senior formal and instead of enjoying the night you are on guard. To his credit, he was forthcoming with you about the people he "dealt" with on campus, which was a smart move on his behalf. You show up for the fashion show practice and were pulled to the side by a few girls, most of whom you knew but never really established any relationship with. Their purpose was to warn you about Shawn, a common theme was "He is nice but does not get serious". Now to most, it would seem they are looking out for you, but you will see it as a red flag. None of these girls are your friends, in fact, they barely spoke on any other day. Miraculously they hear you are talking to Shawn and have so much concern. Now you are thinking, "What is it about this guy?" Most of them have never had any relationship or minimal interaction with him. This appears to be more about them, not you Gem. This interaction becomes irrelevant and a non-factor, instead, you choose to base your opinion on your own experience.

The summer is almost unreal, surprising how well you get along without getting tired of each other. It feels as if something is bound to go wrong, so mentally you decide this won't go past the summer. He has graduated and will be in the "real world", meeting different people and who knows where his path will lead him. Life has been very real for you, especially since the nights you did not stay with him you slept on the floor at your friend's house. Finding ways to fill time until it was late, and you knew someone would be home. Talk about a reality check, this made you feel there can be no distractions, we have no room for error. So, while this summertime dating has been oddly refreshing, allowing you to be free of concern or self-consciousness, this could not go any further. Once September rolled around it was back to campus and you were certain those trips to see him would be less frequent, eventually dying out. But he kept calling and genuinely wanting to see you and spend time. Gem, you have gotten so used to playing the background it was shocking that he still wanted you in his world. It was clear that he could have had any of those girls that called themselves looking out for you, so why you? Being seen is not familiar to you, most times it felt like your mother was the only one to really see your value. Having a father who could not find the time to call for birthdays, show up for special events or show any interest in your overall well-being, really made you feel no man would invest time in you and be careful with your heart. Here we are again waiting for this guy to mess up so you can pack a bag and keep it moving.

One evening you stop at the local diner, and when you walk in there is a girl picking up her order. She turns and sees Shawn and lights up like a Christmas tree, "Hi Shawn". Your radar goes off immediately, especially once he allows you to be seated and stays to speak with her. Once at the table, he explained who she was, he knew it could be nothing more than what it was and that she had some tendencies he did not like. But his actions made it clear what your place was with him. You simply said, "If that is how you feel about her you should be careful, she clearly likes you." He tries to assure you that he made it clear it was nothing more. Gem, we tend to go by actions and not words, but we are willing to see how this plays out.

At the end of September, something feels off, you are very tired and your cycle is late. "Please Lord, tell me I am not pregnant." Taking a test only confirmed your biggest fear and telling him only confirmed it. He gave the classic, "Whatever you want to do I will support you". Which only led you down a rabbit hole of daddy-issue emotions. Fearful that you will bring a child into this world trying to be their everything, only to have an absent father wreak havoc on them emotionally. Gem, what you don't want to do is continue the cycle, it needs to be broken, redefined, and reimagined. So how can we have this baby, especially with someone who has not even tried to ease your mind with worry? Someone who clearly has not really let go of his options. You have no address outside of campus housing, where would you go, and who would help you and be your support? That promise we made Mommy would chatter and what kind of life could you provide without an education? Seems the decision was made for you...

Here comes that bone-shaking thunder, this storm will cause invisible damage. The kind you reflect on quietly, in those moments of reflection and disdain. Pulling up to the door and walking into that building your stomach sinks, everything about this felt wrong. I wanted to turn around; I was second-guessing my decision every minute I waited. Once in the room I wanted to run out but knew no one was waiting to comfort me and tell me not to do this but what other choice did I have? I walked outside and to your surprise, he was waiting. Where were you 30 minutes ago when I needed you to stop me, to tell me "we" cannot do this, to say something that made me feel I was safe with you? Instead, you say less and just thanked him for coming. At this moment you are left feeling empty, a familiar space trying to make sense of another letdown, but this time with yourself.

The holidays were quickly approaching, and it also marks one year since Mommy's death. I wanted to surround myself with family and try to relive the happy times. All of us together, cooking and laughing, allowing for a moment of freedom. Shawn was not happy with this decision, declining his request to be with him for Thanksgiving. But you hoped he understood your need to be with family given the circumstances. However, it was very apparent he didn't once he said he would be spending time with a friend and not to call. Perfect, exactly what I needed, confirmation that you would let me down and at some point, your true colors would show. So, I did exactly as he requested and did not call, you only have to tell me once. My bag was not completely unpacked so it will be really easy to get my things! But something was up, he was different once I returned from seeing my family. He was more attentive and in some ways possessive, which was not in his character. Something happened, but clearly, he was not willing to share. When asked you are told, "When you look for something, you find it." The first thing that came to mind was, the truth always comes to light because I cannot find what is not there!

You spend Christmas and New Year's together, becoming closer and spending just about every weekend together. Valentine's Day rolls around, and for the first time, someone took the time to plan to celebrate loving you. It felt special simply because he took the time to plan a special evening. The best part was the dozen long-stem roses, the whole train ride back to school you felt special. Just thinking about the weekend and how good it felt just to be with him, is this love? These feelings had to be addressed without making him feel he was being forced into a relationship. At the end of a conversation, you ask, "Am I your girlfriend?". His response, "I have never asked anyone out, I usually just end up in a relationship." You let him know right away, "I make no assumptions, so I am not your girlfriend, got it". Just when you thought this might be something, just when you thought his weird behavior might have been an indication of him realizing his feelings, we were back at packing a bag.

What came next, no one could be prepared for. Everything seemed to be perfect, which admittedly scared you. Gem, he asked you to be his girl, something he had never done with anyone. April, he comes to your dorm because he needs to talk with you. Based on his body language and the look on his face you knew it was not good. Here comes that thunder, but this time it shakes you to your core. The words that came next were not anything you could ever prepare for. "I might have a baby on the way." The first thing you ask is, "Is it the girl we saw in the diner?" He answers, "Yes". He shares his recount of how it happened, but it just all seemed irrelevant. You decided to not move forward with a pregnancy, yet he allowed himself to be put in this situation and there is a baby on the way. The thunder now has a continuous rumble the more you think about how he did not consider you in any of this. Nothing left to say, you let him stay in your dorm because it was late, but you just wanted him to go. You knew anything you decided to do from this point has to be based on you, no one else. Needless to say, the vibe is off, the feelings are numb, and he has now given you all you need to zip that bag up.

Weekends continued to be spent together, things seem to go as they were. Your mind is racing and the reality of what might be is becoming a painful reality. He tells you he can handle this relationship and the arrival of a baby. You want to believe him but deep down it is understood that he won't know until it is happening, the real question is will it be worth you staying to find out? It is apparent that you are not the only one struggling with this reality, he clearly is stressed and worried he might lose you. He has been very vocal that he does not want to be with her but could that change when the baby arrives? Gem, you are tired of setting yourself up for letdowns, and having been at your lowest low you will not tolerate being made to feel less than who you finally found yourself to be!

Once the baby arrives, paternity is confirmed, and reality just becomes too overwhelming. Being at the house and seeing the baby regularly, holding her the first time, and looking at her brought on too many emotions, and you are not able to do it. The tears start falling, thinking about the fact that you could be holding your own. This felt like an unexpected lightning strike right before the thunder started to rumble. Shawn follows you and tries to comfort you, understanding your feelings but you know this was just too much. You ask for a break, being honest with yourself, really needing some time to think and be real about how you are feeling. During this time, you continue to speak, and he is very transparent with his feelings and struggles as a new father under the circumstances. It feels like when you first met, no pressure just a natural flow and desire to hear from the other. One day he drives up to the school and asks what he must do, he is willing to do the work. Deciding to give it a try you know that you must come to terms with your decision. Understanding you did what was best based on your circumstance and what you felt was best for that child. This baby has done nothing wrong and did not ask to be here.

As time goes the interactions, comfort level, and ways of the other parental unit caused major conflict. Shawn encouraged you to share your concerns and express how you felt, generally this is something you never were good at because it normally changed nothing. In this situation it appeared it was no different, he would hear you and most times agree but it appeared nothing changed. It felt as if knowing my feelings allowed him to know what to not share so there would be no problem. To me, it felt like he was trying to please too many people. This led to his request for some time apart, he was over the arguments, feeling nothing, he did was enough to satisfy the problem. This time it felt different, it felt final because there was little to no communication. You decide to spend this time figuring out yourself and what would come next. At this point you have a degree and are able to work anywhere, feeling more stable in your ability to earn a living and maintain a household brought a new level of confidence.

Gem, we decided a long time ago that marriage and children were not the options meant for you. Your inability to be vulnerable and trust a man, feeling it was impossible to find value in a union that was destined to be ruined by infidelity and disrespect. You could not knowingly bring children into the world with falsified hopes. The blueprint of a man was severely tainted and warped because the very man who is part of the reason for your existence showed no interest in nurturing your value. We waste no more time on the concept of finding love in a man who will honor your heart, nurture your growth, and find value in your worth. From this point on love is not an option.

Your last words to Shawn were, "Call me when you can tell me what you want." It feels good to be in a place where you feel no obligation and no pain behind letting go. Not that you don't love him, but you are finally starting to see your worth, and compromising was not an option. And if that meant it would not be him that was okay. No storm lasts forever, it eventually runs out of rain and momentum and once it is over, the grass is greener, the sun seems to shine brighter and even the petrichor smell in the air is calming, all symbolizing an awakening. There is so much to be gained from pushing through the hard times, when you run away the opportunity for growth is missed. After graduation, you start working nights, and as you often did when you needed to stay focused, you started working out. It became your new routine to leave work, run to the gym, get a full-body workout, and run home. You were feeling good mentally and physically, and at this point did not give the "break" another thought.

To your surprise, he calls you, trying to have a regular conversation like we didn't just go months with no real communication! Before the conversation went any further you ask, "Do you understand what you want now?" He hesitated for a moment, clearly, he was not prepared for this question. He simply says, "Yes, for us to work on not allowing outside influence to affect us." You ask for time to think but he wants to come and see you. Even though you miss him, we cannot just jump back to what was, so you tell him no. At about 1 am there is a knock at your door, hesitant to answer he says, "D, it's me". Opening the door felt surreal, not sure how to react but it was good to fall asleep in his arms that night. He must have known what giving you time could mean, in your mind the lesson was learned and there were no regrets. Little did you know what was in store.

For him to drive to your house in the middle of the night, to talk and simply hold you really made you think it was worth a shot.

He has got to see something more in you that you don't recognize yet, Gem this is either insanity or the best decision you will make. The routine switches up, you will now drive to his house when you get off work on the weekends instead of working out. This now has you around baby girl more since his mom is watching her during the day. Veggie Tales and Dora the Explorer have become your new favorite shows, and your late-morning naps now have a companion. It became so natural to just be with her and be open to her being with you. Always be careful not to overstep the "mommy" boundary, it still happens, she looks at you and calls you "mom". Of course, you correct her right away and respectfully address it with her mother. There was no real issue with it but did not want to stir up any unnecessary problems. It will not happen again, but the fact that she felt that way emotionally will be enough for you. No way to fully describe how much love you have for this child in your heart, but care must be taken to ensure this does not influence your decision to stay.

No slight to baby girl's mom, but she had her own growth and realities to face to allow herself to move on from the fairytale ending she was hoping for. Shawn understood that getting his own place would help calm some of the situations that would cause problems between us. He brought me with him on his search for a condominium or co-op to purchase, and I was excited for him. Having had the opportunity to have your own little studio apartment, it felt so good to have your own space with no concern for abiding by someone else's rules. Once settled in a one-bedroom co-op, not far from his parents and baby girl, he asks you to move in with him. In your mind, this is major, exciting, and scary. Even after voicing your thoughts on the importance of him having this experience alone, he insists.

Gem, what does this mean? Clearly, he has a plan for you and this will either make or break the relationship.

There is no fairytale to this ending, only work, consistency, and determination. To his credit, it was mostly on the part of Shawn, because the queen of the pack-a-bag tried it. Understanding the complicated nature of being with someone who has a child was more than what you could stand some days. It all will come to a head one Father's Day, no one wants to feel that another would take the time to pick gifts that require so much thought and care into who Shawn is and what he likes. In other words, no woman wants to feel another woman is taking care of her man! So, we do what we do best, pack that bag, Sis. The conflicting energy is the respect you have for the father he is. You wish your father would have made you a priority and taken care in considering what your needs were as a child. There was no way you could ever get in the way of that. Instead of that becoming the case, you thought it best to go. This was a storm you felt you could get away from before it got started well, the thunder was in the distance. You wake up like nothing was different, with greetings, conversation, and well wishes for the day. Once he was gone you packed enough for a few weeks, called his mom and let her know, then called him at the spa treatment that she scheduled and told him to enjoy but you would not be there when he returned. See we were avoiding sharing what might be an issue and are operating in what she doesn't know won't hurt her space. That simply won't work for us Gem because what we require is more than this. Why not book a massage for 2 and cover me or be honest about where you would be? Why the lack of transparency in his actions, thinking you are avoiding a fight or argument, yet creating another issue?

By packing your bag, you created doubt in the mind of the first man to really go the extra mile to show his intent. This action to him now means you could leave at any time if there is another issue that should arise you may not want to confront. He is not running from you; he is trying to grow with you but somehow you keep blocking this opportunity for growth. And not just growth for yourself, but for him and as a couple. See, your mindset is still set to what Daddy did, just waiting for the mess up to justify you leaving. Too worried about not taking any mess and you almost lost the very man who was trying to prove his love to you. The man who was trying to show every man is not unable to keep their word, showing you someone is willing to do the work to make sure you feel the love they have for you is an action. Take a moment to look back and really dissect all the events that led you to this point, it would have been easier for him to walk away than to grow through the pains with you. It only hits you when he says, "I am not your father." The gut punch of pure truth, that not even you could have a response for.

No, he is not prince charming, and yes, he made mistakes that many would find unforgivable. What we had to learn Gem, is there is value in the forgiveness of not just him, but your father and self. You were so busy trying to keep from being with someone like him, you are about to run any man off that makes a mistake. No matter how much their actions show you they are sorry, no matter how they try to grow and become better, your only focus was the issue. This man was never a major part of your life yet seems to be affecting it and your decisions daily. Amazing how the one who was absent holds so much weight in your present. Mommy reminded you every chance she could of your value and worth, she always said it was his loss. Somehow that was not enough, because understanding the why was the missing link. How does someone say they love you, whenever you do see them but can go years without any communication, not even on a birthday? The missing link was not the why, it was for you to stop blaming yourself for the actions of someone else. You were not the problem Gem, he was not able to stand up and be the man his children needed, his selfishness got in the way. In order for you to be loved this has got to be released, stop holding yourself, hostage. There is someone waiting to love you, someone willing to work with you while they are trying to grow into the man you deserve. Some storms are created by self, by our own inability to progress. Because we are unable to move on you are constantly experiencing the same storm, it can never dissipate until you forgive and release. It all originated from the same place of hurt, disappointment, and resentment. This does not protect you from hurt, it will create it!

Over time, what seemed to be a deal breaker was not worth the energy, and what seemed to cause major arguments became a non-factor. The best part is your relationship with the baby girl seems to grow and mature as she does. There are certain things she will come to you for, not that her mom cannot, but because she is comfortable coming to you. It is a different type of love you did not think you were capable of, more so not knowing what this love would look like. The purest form of love comes from a genuine place, without any forced reciprocation or requirements. She has taught you that being yourself is exactly what she needed and loves about you. What is valued most is the innocence and purity in this type of love, no blood ties just God showing that you are deserving of experiencing this type of love. The concerns of how this would work if a bond would develop, would there be an issue with thinking someone else was trying to be her mom; they all were irrelevant because you will take baby girls to lead and just allow love to be the guide. No child asked to be brought into this world, all they require is pure intent with time and care with their heart.

What comes next Gem is set to blow your mind. Shawn accompanies you to visit your mother's grave for the first time on November 15th, 2008, on what would have been her 58th birthday. Stopping at Dunkin Donuts on the way home, your emotions are high it is raining, and cold, and you have not slept. Sitting in the parking lot he starts telling you how much he wants to be by your side and while he cannot fill the void of losing your mother, he wants to be your rock. Of course, you interrupt his speech and let him know you never asked him to fill any voids. Right away he tells you to be quiet and listen. Which only heightened your interest in where he was going with this talk. He tells you he wants you to be his wife, but it did not connect until he pulled out a ring box, followed by "Will you marry me?" Your shock delayed your response, first thing said was "You doing this right now, you are serious? YES!!!" Everything about this moment is not conventional, but that has been the definition of this relationship. Nothing went as ideal but that is what has made the relationship so strong. Marriage and children were not an option for you, at least you thought. Gem, this is a moment that you decided would not happen, simply because you allowed someone else to define your value based on their absence. All you could do is stare at your finger in total disbelief. And then apologize for interrupting your own proposal! This is another moment where he did not fold at your actions and saw past them because he knows your value. While you spent time weathering your storm together and as an individual, he was making plans for you. Learning how to treat you based on what you require.

In full transparency, his faults will force you to confront your fears and his mistakes will force you to accept that you have punished yourself long enough. Life will pass you by if you constantly look for a reason to run. Every mistake does not mean the end, there is healing in forgiveness and power in self-reflection. Growth cannot happen without understanding yourself, without evaluating who you are and why. Be open to love in different forms, you never know how the blessings will come. Your life is not the ideal blueprint, but you will want to change nothing about your experiences and outcome. This does not mean the storms end, but they will be new, and the outcome will bring a better version of yourself because there is power in healing.

This quiet storm of emotions fostered growth and made you take a good look at the punishment placed on yourself. The emotional struggles of your father's absence still linger but the mindset has redefined the approach. The trauma of losing your mother, home, and stability switched you to survival. Pulling from past experiences, and unresolved emotions to find ways to protect yourself from hurt and heighten your awareness of those around you. Today, I am married for 13 years, a mother to 3 children (4 including a baby girl) and I am still quietly weathering my storms. The best part about these storms is no longer allow the aftermath to linger and cause damage. Identify where it comes from, find ways to work through it, grow and release. Forgiveness gives emotional freedom, allowing you to open to the fullness life offers.

Queen

Mel V

When God created woman, he created a masterpiece. Heaven rejoiced at his creation.

What better suited for a queen than to sit on the throne... his Majesty's seat.

Strong and versatile is how he made her, Ready to tackle any task

He placed the crown on her head and said here my daughter,

May these precious jewels adorn your head.

First, he placed an emerald for her leadership and strength.

For teaching those behind her how to exude the pilar of style and grace.

Next, he gave her this ruby and prayed it would always last.

For just like you it endures all things.

Red like the heart you spread so vast.

For being there for others and never missing a beat.

He gave her this sapphire stone.

For her selflessness, empathy, and the sacrifices she's made.

For never letting fear stop her or scare her from what's to come

He gave her this one for courage, now he placed a garnet stone.

For every night she cried on her knees.

Baring her heart and soul

For having faith in him, then the lord placed an amethyst stone

For all the days she thought she couldn't make it

But found a way to push through.

He gave her this pearl, so she'll never forget he created you.

And finally, her crown would not be complete.

without the greatest stone of them all

He gave her a Diamond.

Cuz her love is the greatest gift of them all.

After all the hurt and the pain, her love is still pure and true.

It is the light behind her eyes and the sparkle in her smile too.

Now the lord has placed all the gems and her crown is now complete,

You've earned your place he said, now Queen take your seat.

Ripples

Fionix

Have you ever sat and listened to water? Water has a story to tell. The pitter-patter of raindrops on a window sings a sensual song. Ocean waves washing onto the shore bring tales of adventure from deep below. The roar of a waterfall as it cascades into the waiting pool below commands to be heard. The quiet babbling brook whispers its secrets to all who will listen.

Traveling down from the heavens above to the earth's surface below, water comes in many forms. Think of all it encounters on this journey. What has it seen? What transformations has it gone through? What adventures are still to come?

Gem, you are like water. You can show up in spaces as a quiet storm, calming and relaxing. You can bring with your peace and tranquility. Or you can be a hurricane. Your power pelts everything around you with low vibrational energy leaving a path of destruction in your tail.

Water represents wisdom, emotions, and the ability to move. When we are happy, we cry tears of joy. And likewise, when we experience pain, we release tears of sorrow. Did you know that chemically, those two tears are different? That's because you are like water. Ever changing. Ever shifting. Ever transforming in this cycle of life.

Water is cleansing. Not just in a physical sense, like when it is used to wash away physical debris. But also, in a cosmic and metamorphic sense.

We use water to pour libations and pay homage to our ancestors. Honoring the elders and their wisdom that came before us. We use water in baptism to wash away sin. Powerful streams of heated water can be used to relax tired and achy muscles. Water is magical.

Immerse yourself in the water. Allow the mystic powers to heal and preserve you. Gem, there is potential to do all and be all in water. Think about what occurs when water encounters water. It ripples. Tiny ringlets circle outwards, expanding into bigger rings. The bigger the drop, the bigger and more intense the ripple.

Gem, because you are like water, your energy and everything you do ripples and touches those around you. What effects are you leaving? Expand yourself beyond your wildest dreams. Be magical. Be mystical. Be powerful. Be ever transformative.

Be....WATER.

The Fall of Sam

Suma Leone

There are always three sides to a story...Her side, His side, and then the Truth!

"To discover is to reveal, unmask, and take a step towards seeing the very things that we hide from ourselves. Who am I? What do I want people to know? I am incognito...waiting for my moment of discovery."

Her Side: It was the in thing; made in every color of the rainbow. Most people had it in brown, tan, black, or grey. But, I wanted to stand out in mine — a royal indigo blue Sheepskin Coat with the plushest cuffs would have definitely made me the most popular girl in the 7th grade. With a promise from my Uncle Sam, I was determined to get one that weekend.

We were on our way to Canal Street. It was a cold October morning and the car reeked of Marlboro cigarettes. Ashes and cigarette butts filled the ashtray, while coffee-stained napkins encased the cup holders. I sat in the passenger seat of his 1980 red Chevy Impala. From the radio, Madonna's song, "Material Girl" comforted me as I giddily sang along. Looking out of the passenger window, in and out of my subconscious mind, I daydreamed about how "funky fresh" I would look in my royal indigo blue Sheepskin Coat.

A sea of fallen leaves covered the city parks where kids jumped and played in the crunchy cacophony of a red, orange, yellow, and brown array of leaves. "We have to make a stop!", he mumbled and I snapped back to reality. We weren't on Canal Street — we were still in Brooklyn, across the street from his Fort Greene apartment on St. James Place. Uncle Sam nodded and motioned for me to come upstairs with him. Staring at him in awe and confusion I stuttered, "Don't worry Uncle Sam...I...I can just wait for you in the car." In his deep raspy voice he howled, "I left my wallet upstairs and need to make a phone call, now let's go!" There was a long pause, and then a deep sigh, before the feeling of a swarm of bees stung my stomach in turmoil. I leaned over slowly to unlock the door handle, which seemed to take forever.

I grudgingly walked towards his two-story brownstone apartment. It was a walk-up and unlike my parent's house, the kitchen and bathroom were located in the hallway, on the outside of his apartment. He shared this space with a retired police sergeant. Waiting for him to rummage through his sticky keys, the stench permeating from the quarter-sized hole in the wall made me want to vomit. He finally got the door open.

A tiny one-room apartment with a small refrigerator straight ahead, leopard skinned shaggy rug in the center, and a king-size waterbed to my left, he meticulously took my coat off and placed it on the back of a weathered leather recliner to my right. This gesture immediately created an atmosphere of panic. He walked over towards his closet where he removed a huge brown store bag. "I have a surprise for you!" Still, in a state of disillusionment, I wondered what it could be. Like a slow-motion movie, he pulled out a sheepskin coat. What's worse is that it wasn't even royal blue indigo with the plushy cuffs. It was gray with specks of brown, which looked like a scruffy old and decrepit hyena. That shit was absolutely atrocious!

My eyes slowly welled up with tears as the warm fluid rolled down my cheeks, creating glistening tracks down my face. I was instantly transported to my ancestral homeland of Sierra Leone, where ceremonial rites of passage mimicked tribal marks. What was this rite that was about to take place? I am only 12. With a slow and deliberate motion, he sat me down on the water bed. It was odd as my body moved to the motion of the waves. I was a virgin to both the bed and the actions I felt were soon to follow. Every single beat seemed to push me further into a state of fear and imprisonment. As I struggled to hear his words, my heartbeat resonated against my eardrums.

The revelation of dreams I can't see.

A headache ensued as my eyes fought to make sense of his actions.

The sensation of rose thorns I can't feel. I could only feel my heartbeat against my chest.

The conversation of words I can't hear. All sense of hearing was lost.

The admission of triumph I can't taste. I could only taste the warm blood as I bit my lip in agony.

The sweet aroma of the rose I can't smell. The devastation of innocence is no longer mine to keep.

That Monday morning in homeroom class felt different. As my teacher called my table number, I confidently walked with my hideous grey sheepskin coat towards the coat closet. As I placed it on the top hook, I seemed so far removed from the little boys at my desk; that I played "Hide n' Seek" with them during recess, the Friday before. I held my head up high, took a deep breath, and prepared to expose myself to the world. As I turned around to face the class, I felt the bruises from the imprints that Sam had left on my arms. It was at that moment that reality hit me – the discovery that I had become a woman.

Uncle Sam is Watching

There are always three sides to a story...Her side, His side, and then the Truth! "When love shuts its doors you become vulnerable, exposed, alone; with nowhere to run, and nowhere to hide. In a maze of deception, deceit, and hurt, you fall victim to your own demise. When love shuts its doors, the feelings of hate can mask the misty fog. When love shuts its doors, time will reveal the man in the mirror."

His Side: When was the last time you looked into the mirror and felt totally content with what you saw? Not an inkling of guilt, dissatisfaction, shame, or disgust. No man is flawless, although we often wear the cloak of perfection. I was her hero. I had everything she wanted and needed, I supplied. I was invincible. There was nothing I could not do or do well enough in her eyes. Her love for me was pure. With her, I never worried about saying the wrong thing or upsetting her. She lived to please me without question. She worshiped me -- and my words echoed like lines from the scriptures. When others saw a monster, she saw a God. Our love is perfect, I thought to myself as we walked up the stairs; I loved the innocence of it all and the control that she relinquished to me. She often jumps into my arms as soon as she can possibly reach me, making me feel wanted and needed. So many women have proven to me that I am not worthy of their love, but today, I feel loved by her and it's time for me to express it back.

I slowly open the door to my tiny one-room apartment and lead her in. She walks awkwardly to my room as if it is a foreign land.

Her facial expression reveals a slight uneasiness as the stench permeating from the quarter-sized hole in the wall made contact with her pudgy nose. I beckon her to sit on my king-size waterbed. Her unstable gait and fidgety steps expose her fear and discomfort of being here with me, alone. I look into her innocent eyes. I slowly remove my cloak and release it to the ground. Her jaw dropped as her eyes made contact with mine. I gently laid her back on the bed and mounted her. She began to cry. Before she could utter a word, my lips muffled her "NO!" Lost in the abyss, we swam like poetic perfection...

Minutes had only gone by when lust personified.

My shivers turned overwhelming.

Desires of acting out realistic fantasies forced me to lose control.

I truly, wholeheartedly wanted and had to have you.

This need metamorphosed into orgasmic explosions.

Leaving their mark inscribed.

Can I contain this unrestrained?

Sexual craving

That slowly seems to guide me down a delirious path.

A part of me wants to exert this intensity onto your soul and body.

Letting it surge through you.

Another part of me wants to suppress these overflowing desires.

Afraid of the chaos it may create.

Awakened by her cries, I returned to my reality. I slowly got up and walked out to the bathroom located in the hallway, on the outside of the apartment. I shut the door! My back remained glued to the door as if I thought that someone would come running to pry it open. I took two steps to the sink, slowly turned on the faucet, and allowed the cold water to run into the palms of my hands. I slowly brought my face down into the meeting of my palms. The cold water sent chills running down my spine. I raised my head strategically so as to only reveal the parts of my face that I was ready to see.

Similar to a dark sunrise, I saw my hairline, my forehead, and my eyebrows, followed by the erratic flutter of my eyelids -- then the eyes. The eyes were what caught me. As they stared back at me all at once I saw the devil in the flesh. Suddenly I felt guilty, ashamed, and disgusted. What kind of man am I? She's only twelve. Save me from myself.

The Truth

"When the Spirit of truth comes, He will guide you into, all the truth, for He will not speak on His own authority, but whatever He hears, He will speak, and He will declare to you the things that are to come." John 16:13ESV

At 50 years old, I am still haunted by that sunny day. After five children and two failed relationships, I still feel the scars, though invisible to the human eye. Looking for love in all the wrong places has deemed me ruined, broken, and damaged. But when I found Jesus, He washed my sins, my hurt, and my pain. He filled the void that I have needed since the age of 12. When I look back at the Bible, the number 12 holds great significance. There were 12 disciples of Jesus, 12 Tribes of Judah, the woman who had an issue with blood bled for 12 years, Jairus' daughter was raised by Jesus from the dead, at the age of 12, and now I can add myself to that repertoire of greatness. I was 12 when my innocence was taken from me, but the love of my God, my Lord, my Savior paved the way to accept Him and embrace Him. I love a man today, who is a Kingdom Man, one who loves God more than himself, and so he can love me and my children in a healthy and honorable way. I thank God for his love, kindness, and generosity. I no longer search for love to fill my void, I found God and He found me. He has never left my side nor forsaken me.

Lost

Mel V

Fumbling through my thoughts with no clear direction. Completely misunderstood by self. Unsure of which thoughts are true but absolutely mesmerized with the idea. Is there love or has it been dried up and left destitute like the terra incognita of Egypt? Has it been abandoned or is the seed firmly planted beneath the dirt fortified with hope... waiting... for that isolated raindrop to inseminate its growth.

A reflectionless Reflection of a mystery that too many have viewed but none have seen. A painted picture all in white, so effortlessly wrapped in a golden frame. A deep gasp for air amidst the water. A Navy ribbon in a black sky. A pre-conception of a misconception of a believable fallacy that is nothing more than truth.

I sit again, fumbling through my thoughts as if knowing my destination but having no clear direction. Why have you consumed this space? Did you not see the sign? No vacancies... Max capacity reached but you... as disrespectful as a mannerless child have set up shop here. Disregarding the necessary precautions and doing what you do too well... with your mischievous, lackluster demeanor you have strolled your ass into my no-fly zone and fuck shit up. You, you, you...

I, I sit here fumbling, through this invisibly visible, misconstrued understanding of a fallacy that is life.

Grounded

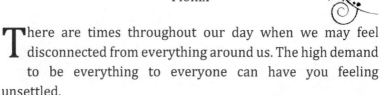

Fionix

There are times throughout our day when we may feel disconnected from everything around us. The high demand to be everything to everyone can have you feeling unsettled.

It is in these intense moments we must pause and take the time to get ourselves grounded and recentered. We must remind ourselves that in our lives, there are going to be things that we have little to no control of. We can only control our reactions and responses.

The element of earth seeks rootedness and stability. Its purpose is to ground and bring harmony.

As children, many of us ran carefree through the grass in tune with nature. Whether it was in our own yards or a park, the feelings we experienced being connected to the earth were one of pure joy and liberty.

Gem, I invite you to return to that time. Let us use our five senses and take a trip back to when we were young and unbothered.

Where are you? Where did you go?

What do you see? Who are you with? Friends, family, or are you by yourself?

Can you taste nature? What do you feel on your tongue? What does it taste like?

What do you hear? Is it the animals that live in this glorious place? How about the sounds of laughter? Is it yours or someone else's?

What does it smell like? Is it the distinctive aroma of freshly cut grass? Or the wonderful fragrance of flowers?

Lastly, what are you touching? Do your feet tickle from blades of grass sliding between your toes? Do you feel the firmness of the solid ground from a trail or path?

Gem, what is happening in your body right now? I encourage you to recognize and connect with what is happening inside of you. This is what it feels like to get recentered and ground in yourself. Honor your body and all that is happening to it both physically and spiritually.

You are a divine creation made with a purpose. Know that no matter how similar your destination is to someone else's, you will walk your own path. This is not a road trip. To get to your whole self you will need to stay rooted in YOUR mission and vision. Do not allow outside distractions to throw you off your foundation. Stay grounded in your awareness. Be rooted and grounded within yourself.

Allow the harmony and stability of your ability to be grounded to be the foundation of all you do to all those you touch in your lives.

Features

Lady J.A

Images of me... frustrated me. I see him in me, and it makes me hate me. Blame me. Dislike me.

The more I look, the more I see him in me.

What I hoped could not be.

Almond eyes.

The mole in the center of my back... raised and dark, in the same spot as he.

The vein that runs down the forehead.

Curvature of the feet.

The posture. The stance.

Yet he never thinks of his vital role... never making time for me.

The absent party holds so much weight.

The mystery behind where he might be.

What could be so important that it keeps him from me?

The absence and lies... those cannot be family ties.

Trying to change something about me, to no longer remind me of who he could not be.

Reminders of love I longed to feel, held myself accountable for what he should be.

Wondering what I could do to make him want to be a part of me... as I am he.

The Purpose of An Unplanned Pregnancy

Dyisha Lewis

Dear Gem,

Life happens and it can happen fast! Imagine living your best life, traveling, and having fun without a care in the world; well, other than bills of course. I just described myself when I was in my mid to late twenties. I had started teaching at a private school in MD and loved my students, co-workers, and the direction my life was headed. I was really focusing on my relationship with God, studying the Bible, and taking classes to become a Minister, then life happened. I discovered I was pregnant. Let me tell the story. I loved to sleep (I think we need naptimes at work) and it got to the point where I felt like I had never been asleep after a nap. I used to work out with our school track team, running bleachers and everything else with no problems. I was in a relationship and life was great! I mentioned how I felt tired after waking up from a nap or even after 8 hours of sleep to a co-worker and she told me to take a pregnancy test to rule out being pregnant. I went and bought the test thinking it was going to come back negative. Boy was I wrong! I took five tests at home and had an excuse each time it was positive. I cried and prayed to God telling Him I would never have sex again if He let the test come back negative. Even after test number five, I thought there was still a chance the test was wrong. I mean, there have been occasions where a pregnancy test was incorrect. This was the story I kept telling myself. So, I decided to go to the free clinic, and when the nurse came around the corner with a teddy bear and said,

"Congratulations," my heart sank. I was in such disbelief, that after I stopped by my godmother's house, I had to figure out what I wanted to do. I didn't have that feeling of joy most woman experience when they find out they are expecting. I should have been happy, on cloud nine, ecstatic, but I wasn't. I mean, growing up I never wanted kids and it was well-known by all who knew me! Truth be told, I didn't even like kids really. Now, I had a decision to make that I wasn't ready for, and still couldn't believe this was happening. My life was about to change forever, regardless of my decision.

So many questions ran through my mind! Am I ready to have a baby right now? Do I even want to have this guy's child? Will I still be able to accomplish my personal and professional goals? Can I do this by myself? What will the father think when I tell him? How will my family respond? I mean, this was not part of the plan I had for my life at this time. I was getting ready to go to Jamaica for my cousin's wedding! Actually, the father noticed me getting a little stomach before I found out and my response was, "Yeah, need to work out to get bikini ready for this wedding!" Again, getting a bikini-ready was not about to happen! After keeping this to myself for a long time, I finally said something to the father. I didn't know how to let him know he was going to be a father. We had a conversation about kids in general and whether we wanted any (whether we were together or not). This was just a conversation we had as we were getting to know one another. Still trying to come to terms with the fact I was about to be responsible for another human, part of me understood I was going to have to tell him and soon. He had just had surgery and I tried to tell him in a riddle, "What starts with P and ends with T?" He had no idea! I blurted out, "I'm pregnant!" It was quiet at first because I think he was in shock and mind you he was recuperating from a surgery he had just had and was high on pain meds. We had the conversation again when he was not on pain meds and discussed our plan. The father and I hadn't been together that long, and we were still getting to know each other. He was all in and wasn't even second-guessing what he wanted to do. However, I still was not sure I wanted to keep this child. Honestly, I really didn't give a shit. I was still thinking about how my life plans were now interrupted by this human growing inside of me. Oh, and by the way, I found out in the middle of my second trimester. Now, if you're wondering, I still hadn't said a word to my parents. I mean, I was the child who did everything by the book, except for getting pregnant out of wedlock. I mean, I stopped everything at church as it related to being a minister because of the guilt and shame I felt. I mean nobody knew except the few people I told. In June, I, along with my father, went to my cousin's graduation party in NC. He wanted to tell my dad then, but I refused. The thing is, my dad was visiting his mom and when he visits, he is completely about his mother. I didn't feel it was the right time, besides I told him that wasn't how he wanted to be introduced to my dad. We went back to MD after the graduation festivities, and I called and told my brothers' and the oldest told me to send a singing telegram. I laughed. I couldn't believe he suggested that, although I was still struggling with how to tell them they were about to be grandparents again. So, I ended up telling my dad via text message. That's how ashamed I was, I couldn't even speak it! I ignored my dad's call and everything, and how ironic, I was on my way to Bible study! Honestly, I can admit that I was angry at God for allowing me to become pregnant and the father for not using proper protection during sex. I was even angry with the baby in my womb for derailing the life plans I painstakingly put together.

Gems, If you have just discovered that you are pregnant, and you hadn't planned it, then you need to accept that you are in shock, with feelings ranging from being thrilled and delirious to being negative and confused. This is a phase that you should try to accept, and then wait for the most intense emotions that have surfaced to subside, after a few days. Allow yourself to experience the rollercoaster of emotions, accepting them and letting them come and go, as they will. Be aware of feelings that trigger actual physical reactions in you, and pay special attention to those ones. Having mixed feelings is allowed. I gave myself permission to feel every emotion. Somehow, I had to find peace with the situation. I remember when I found out I was expecting, I was scared, shocked, and mad at myself for not being more careful. Everybody that knows me knew I never wanted kids, I didn't even like them (outside of being related to them). It wasn't until that first ultrasound visit and I heard that heartbeat and saw that face, that I knew I had to keep the baby. I fell in love. I was still scared; felt I would suck as a parent and worse thought the baby wouldn't love me. All I knew was that I wanted my body back and for this to be over! Who knew that my daughter would save me, I know I didn't! God knew what I needed before I did! I learned a lot during this process! I got married to her father, we got divorced and now we have the best co-parenting relationship ever. I've given myself grace and I have peace with everything I've gone through so far on this journey.

Though you may feel like you're spiraling, it's important to remember that someone else has experienced the exact same feelings—perhaps even more deeply! From fear to dread and inadequacy to hopelessness, you are not alone. There are people out there that understand what you're dealing with and are more than willing to journey with you. I am thankful for the village I had along my journey. I was still teaching, albeit at a new school, but even they were supportive. Truth be told, a few of my students told me the names of a few shows my daughter would really enjoy based on what their younger siblings watched. I took note and she loved every show they mentioned. Although at the time I started teaching, I really didn't like kids, they didn't know that. I showed love regardless and still regard them as my "babies!" I believe teaching was preparing me for what God had in store, I just didn't realize it at the time. Part of my fear was, how was I going to be able to love this child and raise her to the best of my ability. The good thing about it was her father was all in! This was going to be both of our first children. Clueless about what to expect, we prepared for her arrival. Just a side note, God gives us what we need, not necessarily what we want! I learned that when I found out I was pregnant. It was confirmed in the middle of my second trimester! I went four and a half months not knowing I was carrying another human!! That was so crazy to me! My eating habits never changed, until the pregnancy was confirmed. At that point, I could only eat her godfather's cooking, he was part of our village. I was already taking care of myself, but he made sure we ate healthily, and we are glad! I always heard people say, "You're never really ready to have kids." I didn't know what it meant until life happened to me. Even if a child is planned, I don't think you can really be "ready."

The fear, anger, and isolation you're experiencing make the journey ahead of you feel dark and uncertain, a trek you're unsure you're willing or even able to make. But this is the beauty of community, a village—you never have to find your way alone. Whether friends, family members, fathers, churchgoers, neighbors, or counselors, you have access to others who will cry with you, rejoice with you, go to appointments with you, make dinners for you, including you, and enter the trenches of pregnancy with you. Your next 60 years may not look the same, but life's deepest blessings often spring from the most unexpected of gifts. Motherhood is not cookie-cutter! Your experience will be different from the next. Speak freely about your experiences, the highs, and the lows, the joys and sorrows, but most of all the lessons you learned. I wish I would have known that journaling your thoughts and emotions was another great way to regulate your feelings and assess them more extensively. Once the intensity of the shock has waned, you'll be better situated to go back to these notes and evaluate. You'll likely find that while some of your fears remain very real and profound, others don't seem as important. If you find there are some fears that still linger, get counseling! There is nothing wrong with seeking help! Unresolved fears and issues can lead to anxiety and a state of depression. Again, you are not alone Gems! There are many that have gone before you on this journey and many will follow. All that I have gone through and all that I will face, the enemy wants me to give up. But, with all God has called me to be, I see why the enemy would want me to quit. I still don't believe I have a whole teenager! I still have my moments where I think to myself, "Am I doing a good job raising this young Queen?" Sometimes, I feel like I've failed when she experiences things I didn't but tried to guide her in a way she would avoid peer pressure. I cry and pray about it, then realize she has to learn and experience things on her own. She is growing up and like most teens, "parents don't know anything!" I wouldn't trade this journey, nor her, for the world! It's funny how I see bits and pieces of her father and myself. As she's gotten older, she looks like both of us, but in the beginning, there was no hope she looked just like her dad. Our village has gotten bigger as she has gotten older. She has so many "aunties", "cousins", and "siblings," it's not even funny. Gems, we must keep going and pressing through the storm, whatever that may be! Don't worry about what other people think or say, they don't have a Heaven or Hell to put you in! Build a village or what some consider a support system, even if it doesn't include family and friends. There are people out there willing to help you! Had I given up and aborted my daughter, my purpose would have died along with her. There is a great purpose that lives inside of you, remember you have a village that cares for and loves you! You are not alone! We are here for you, with no judgment. This pregnancy didn't ruin your life; it just changed it. It's going to be okay. I promise.

Black Excellence

Mel V

I am the unimaginable imagination of creativity that flows thru every fiber of your being.

I am the blue ribbon in a black sky the painted picture all in white I am the unconceivable

I am the abstract strokes of your paintbrush and the graceful plies and arabesque floats.

I am the rhythmic curves of your tongue, The roaring percussion of your heartbeat, the melodic Symphony of your soul.

I am that captured moment, that precious dream, the uncultivated resilience of everything put against me.

I am hope

I am life

I am light.

I am everything they said I couldn't be

I am the unthinkable.

I am you

I am me.

We are the black excellence.

Forged By Fire

Fionix

Welcome gem to a new season of growth and transformation. As you begin to manifest yourself into this "improved" version of self, you may begin to feel affliction. That is because, with any type of growth, renewal, or expansion, there is discomfort.

Where do you feel that dis-EASE? What is burning inside of you? Is it your head, as your brain is working in overdrive? Are you finding yourself constantly clearing your throat because you have now discovered the power of your voice and self-expression? Or do you feel the fire in the pit of your belly as it warms your soul? Where is the heat?

There is a certain level of awareness one must possess to become an improved version of themselves and birth a new existence. A shift in consciousness occurs that ignites a deeper INNERstanding of self. Nobody knows you, like you know you.

At this point, you have become a trailblazer with a mission and purpose. Others are beginning to see YOU as a beacon. Your inner light is shining through and casting away fear, doubt, and pain. It is exposing you to bravery, confidence, and healing.

The element of fire symbolizes love, power, strength, and energy. Take this time to assess your life. Who or what do you love? Where do you draw your strength and power from? With whom or what and where do you spend your energy? Are you reciprocated? Do you get back what you put in?

Step into the fire gem. While fire has the ability to destroy, it also has the ability to forge. This means it has the ability to create. To sharpen. To shape whatever, it is exposed to.

You have everything within you to manifest whatever it is you desire. All you must do is embrace the power of the fire you possess.

Overcoming Hurt

Lena E

Dear Gem,

No one said that life was going to be easy. There is the good, the bad, and the ugly. The key is how you respond to the heartache, disappointment, and violation that others will cause you that counts. I have been hurt by so many people that I stop counting. I refuse to let the hurt from my family, first marriage, and closest friends weigh me down. There is one verse that I live my life by that helps me overcome and heal, Philippians 4:13 I can do all things through Christ who strengthens me.

This is not one of those he hurt me and now I hate man stories. It is quite the opposite. Yes, I was in a bad marriage, and I gave my ex-husband over 22 years of my life. He lied, cheated, and wasted my money and my resources. All I had to show for it was my two beautiful daughters. The one thing that was constant in my life was that I was a church girl. My family was one of the families that helped build the church, so we were very involved with the ins and outs of the church. I was raised being voluntold (volunteer/told) for everything in the church. We went to church every day. Regular service on Sunday, Member meeting on Monday, cleaning the church on Tuesday, bible study on Wednesday, Thursday night was choir practice, Friday night was young people night, Saturday was neighborhood outreach and trips days. I was raised in the church, so I knew how to pray. I asked God to give me strength and to make me a better version of myself for my children. His reply was self-care. To become a better version of myself I had to take care of myself first. For all my life I had always put everyone before myself. I had put all my efforts and my energy into my marriage and my children, but I never took care of myself.

Working On Me

To become a better version of myself I had to get to know myself. I had to get in touch with myself. See I had become a girlfriend, then a wife, and a mother, and which each role I took on I lost a part of who I was. Who am I, what did I like, and what made me happy were the questions that I asked myself. I then began to start doing things for myself. I dated myself and began to fall in love with myself. Now, this may sound weird to some people who don't know about self-care. It is more than just getting your hair and nails done. Self-Care is treating yourself with the same love and respect that you show to your family and close friends. It's about taking care of yourself physically, emotionally, socially, spiritually, and personally, your home environment, finances, and your professional life. If you don't take the time to take care of yourself, you will wake up one day hating your life and slowly resenting everyone in it. Getting up every day on autopilot takes care of everyone and everything around you emotionlessly. Well, it's time to stop.

Physical care consists of getting enough rest, eating healthily and simply getting some fresh air. Then you must pay attention to your emotions by making sure that you are ok by listening to some music, writing in a journal, or even doing some artwork or seeking professional help when needed. You also need a healthy social life. Be very careful whom you select to be in your personal circle, not everyone is for you. This is done by spending time with others, for example, your family and friends. Go out and have some fun. You must also feed your spiritual side by praying, meditating, and physically going to your place of worship. Then there is personal care where you must honor who you are and what you enjoy. Not your children or spouse but you and you are alone. The home environment is to create a clean and safe space for yourself and your family. I don't allow any negative vibes in my home. I must deal with enough in the world. As for me and my household, we will serve the Lord. I know I had to get my finances to provide for myself and my children. Living from paycheck to paycheck was no longer an option. To do this, I had to find a job where I could be productive and feel valued.

Taking Care of My Family... We are Not A Statistic

I worked three jobs to make sure that I could provide everything for my girls. One income in the state of Florida was not enough to run a household. I had 2 full-time jobs, and I did Lyft in my spare time. The income from my work-from-home job was to cover the house requirements. (Rent, groceries, and utility bills) My second full-time job was to cover investments and sayings, and Lyft was to extras money for going out to eat and family activities. Everyone I knew in Florida had a regular 9 to 5 and a side hustle.

I am Jamaican so getting food stamps and help from the government was not an option. I work a full 40 hours at home. I work from home because I wanted to be there physically for my children. I wanted to get them ready for school, then take them off the bus while having a snack ready for them. I wanted to help them with their homework while they told me about their day at school. I believe in a hot dinner every night. Once they did homework and settled in for the night. Then I left for my security job at night a 42-hour shift (3 nights at 12 hours and ½ nights) and on the nights I did not do security I was out doing Lyft making $600 to $800 a week. The jobs in my area that I went to school for required me to leave home and drive into the heart of Orlando. The time spent driving to and from work would have me worry about my children and my body could not handle that kind of stress. My first and most important job was to be a mother first. My ex-husband worked off the books so there was no child support for me to collect.

Many asked how did you do it all? Well, I had a system on my day off from the at-home job I would clean, do laundry, and cook a week's worth of food. All my girls had to do was warm it up. I put my girls on a private bus that would pick them up from the front door and bring them back home when school was over. I would always pray and ask God to put people in my life to assist me. I love my girl's bus driver. She was also from up north and a single mom so she would watch them open the door. They would then wave to and close the door before she pulled off. In the morning she would honk and if she didn't see that front like come on in less than a minute, she would call them to make sure they were up and coming outside. Yes, my first grader had a cell phone, and her sister did too. I made sure that the principal and teachers knew so please don't take their phones away. I did not have time to come to the school to pick them up. Our cell phones were our lifeline. My girls knew that when they saw mommy calling, they better answer them or else.

I include my children in running the household. I refuse to run myself into the ground cleaning up after them. No, they are not too young to help around the house. I assigned things based on their age. I explained to them that we all had responsibilities and that for us to be successful we had to work as a team. No one was to be laying down while the other was cleaning, they had to do it together. I told them that they had to respect each other and listen to one another and always respect each other's feelings. Most importantly they were to always have each other back.

Family time was a bit different in our home. We love family time and going out to eat. On my night off we would have a movie night in my room. We made finger foods, and everyone would pick a movie. We had cable and all the movie channels. You guessed it I would make it to the first movie and fall asleep. I would wake up in the middle of the second and most of the third. My girls never complain. They would just snuggle up next to me because they always put me in the middle. After church on Sundays, we would go out to eat. The girls would oversee picking the restaurant.

I did involve my children in some of the decision-making and maintaining the home. They were responsible for keeping their room clean, doing their laundry, cleaning the kitchen at night (no dirty dishes in my sink overnight), and their bathroom. I didn't pay my kids for cleaning the home because that was their responsibility. I would have them pick from cleaning the house on Friday when they got home from school or early Saturday morning. They would always pick Friday to get it out of the way so that they could sleep late on Saturday morning. We would have monthly meetings where they would bring any concerns to me and anything coming up for school like picture day and field trips. However, when it was report card season A's was $10, and B's was $5. Jazzy, my oldest was responsible for family vacations she would research where they wanted to go, how much it would cost, and so forth. Gabby was five years younger than Jazz so her input even small was very important to the family like Mom why can't we use paper plates and bowls? Which I did implement. But most importantly, I was always honest with my children. If they asked for something and I didn't have it at that time I would tell them.

When it was tax season, I would divide my refund into four groups. The first group was for a family vacation. I worked hard so we had to play harder. The Second group was for school. It covered school supplies, uniforms, field trips, etc. The third group was for investments which consist of putting money in their mutual funds, stocks, bank accounts, and the petty cash that we kept in the house. The last groups were bills/house. I would pay for my car insurance for six months at a time. I would pay a little extra on my light bill because in those summer months no matter what you did the light bill always went up. I stocked the house with groceries. I always have two deep freezers in my home, one full of meat and the second with frozen snacks for my girls. It would have French fries, hamburgers, hot dogs, hot pockets, and other things of that nature. I would also stock my house with house essentials like toilet paper, laundry soap, etc. Did I mention that I was also an extreme couponer?

You Will Get Married Again

People would see me and say you are so happy, and I would reply I am stress-free and man free. Men would approach me and say you are a good woman you and your daughter always look so nice and happy, and I would reply yes with a smile. Let me pause right here to see. I worked hard and I played harder. I would take two to three cruises a year with my girls. In the summertime, they would go to Jamaica to spend time with my mother and my family that was living out there. We ate the best, I drove the best and you could see God's blessing all over my life. When we went to the hairdresser, I was looking at $300 to $600 on getting our hair done. I would go shopping and did not have to look at the price. I had started mutual funds for my daughters as well as for myself, I was buying stock and bonds and timeshares I was living my best life I had to maximize my singleness. Nobody could tell me shit.

One Sunday there was an alter call and the spirit led me to go. With my hands raised, what is that they said, "Marriage again "Who me oh no not that shit again. I had already done that they got the wrong one. I had already given 22 years out of my life that I could never get back. We are good. My girls have the newest clothes, and the latest technology. I don't need any man to help me raise my babies. I had complete control over my household and my finances. I was fixing my credit and getting the house ready. I had money in the bank. What did I need a man for?

My friends would say don't you get lonely. I was like No! I had a bag of tricks to entertain myself. Or they would ask don't you miss a warm body next to you. Sure, I did so in the summertime when my girls were in Jamaica momma would have a fling or two, but I would let them know that come August the 1st you no longer exist. Don't call my phone or text me. I refuse to bring anyone men around my girls. I was the friend in high school that always had a boyfriend or two. Marlene was never man free, so it was weird for me not to be in a relationship. But I knew that I had to take some time to myself before I rushed into another relationship because I felt lonely or the pressure from others. I had to get my mind right first. I had a lot of anger and bitterness going on inside. I didn't want to take my anger and frustration out on another person that was not deserving of it.

I ran from dating like the plague. The more I ran the more my friends would try to hook me up with someone. Come over for game night they said and there was always an extra person for me. I was never rude, but rather very polite, and funny. I am Leo; I was always the life of the party. I even went to pick up my daughters from Jamaica and my mom was like Tanisha I have someone for you. I was so over it.

I finally gave in because I am a God-fearing woman, and I did not want to be disobedient. So, I prayed to God like how I am talking to you right now. If it is your will for me to get married again, I need some things. My biggest fear was not a man hurting me again but how they treated my girls. God chose me to be their mom. My first job in this world is to protect them until they can protect themselves. The last thing I wanted to do was to bring someone into our home and lives that would cause harm on any level. My girls are my treasures and prize possessions. My children are my world. In my darkest moments, it was my love for them that brought me out. They are the driving force that pushes me every day and made me the warrior that I am today.

I began my research on marriage. I needed to get it right this time. I looked up every verse and chapter in The Bible on marriage. I did not want another failed marriage. I listen to a lot of ceremonies by Dr. Myles Munroe. Two books that I suggest are "The Purpose and Power of Love & Marriage" and" Single Married Separated & Life After Divorce". Seeing my first marriage I felt like I did nothing wrong. While doing my research I realized what I did wrong, and I had to take responsibility for what I did. I de-man my husband. I only paid all the bills and spoiled him rotten. My ex-husband did not have to work. I wasn't his wife I became his mother. He had no responsibility and no accountability. I never let him become the head of the household. I did not demand anything from him. I never activated him into husband mode. Our relationship started when we were children, I was 16 and he was 19. We were playing house without a manual.

Understanding The Roles of a Husband and Wife In Marriage

I started to make a list of what I wanted my future husband to be and to have and so forth and the Holy Spirit stop me and said," I maximized your singleness, so now it was time for your covering... your husband. That is the purpose of having a husband in your life.

I wasn't sure what the covering was, so I did my research, and it blew my mind. I had to take my time with this. 1 Peter 3:7" Likewise, you husband, dwell with them according to knowledge, give honor to the wife, as to the weaker vessel, and as being heirs together of the grace of life: that your prayers be not hindered. "The role of the husband is to be the protector of the family. He is responsible for the livelihood and survival of the family. The husband is to protect his wife in every aspect. For example, it is his responsibility that she has a good car to get around in. When she has any type of business venture, he is like her lawyer to help read over the contract and so forth. He gets her what she needs even if it is not in his skill set or area of expertise. He looks out for her to make sure that she is not walking into any dangerous traps set by the enemy or other humans. Wives are to submit to their husbands and by doing so we are trusting in their leadership as he is the head of the household. God is the main covering, and he is guiding the home in the direction it needs to go.

A husband being a wife's covering does not mean that he is dominating or controlling but the opposite he respects her. A husband that doesn't honor his wife God sees that and will not answer his prayers. If a man is not ready to cover a woman, he should not marry. God's purpose for a marriage is that a home be healthy and strong, it's not always perfect but God requires that two people commit to his standards of a Godly union and a godly home. I felt a sense of peace after I read this with understanding. See in this game called Life we have roles, and we need to understand what position we play and the requirements.

The husband is to cover by protecting the wife from harm on every level. I am not supposed to be out here trying to be a husband and a wife all by myself. My husband is to take the burden off my back. Have you ever had a bad day and you get home to that man in your life, and you tell him you need a hug, and he puts those arms around you and holds you until the day melts away? Stay in that moment his arms are covering you and you feel so safe that you surrender to the strength in his arms as you nuzzle your nose in his neck to breathe in his essence. I was like I am ready God what do you require of me? I had to submit it to my husband. I had been the head of my household for so long that I struggled with the idea of giving someone else complete control. Will he understand all my financial needs and how I wanted my house to function? Then I had to trust that he was going to take care of me and our children. That he is going to go hard for us every day and that God is in control. Trusting that this man is not going to cheat on me, disrespect me, or abuse me in any way and God said yes. A wife is not just for cooking or cleaning. They are the gatekeepers of their husbands' hearts. When God calls you to be a wife, he is trusting you with the well-being and maintenance of that man's heart. So please my sister be very careful with that man's heart.

A Letter for My Husband

Always be very specific about what you ask God for. So, I wrote God a letter that became my prayer for my future husband. It went like this since I am to marry again, let him know first that I am to be his wife because Lord I might self-sabotage it if you tell me that he is supposed to be my husband first. I also didn't have time to waste, just send me my husband. I didn't want to be on the never-ending dating wheel. Also, God grooms him to be my husband as you groom me to be his wife. I need this man to love my children as if they are naturally his. I also did not want a man with any prior children I wanted to give him his first child. I didn't want any baby mama drama. I need him to love me unconditionally despite my flaws. Let us not only be able to build a family together but a business as well. I want to leave a legacy for our children. I need him to be tailor-made just for me. Let him be financially sound and want to be the head of my household because I am a strong woman so let him not be threatened by my strength but see it as an asset. Let him be kind, loving, playful, and passionate. You know me, Lord. Let him always be able to keep a smile on my face and a song in my heart. Let me not harm or disrespect him. If we have any disagreements let us be able to sit down and resolve them in a calm manner. Amen. The only thing that I did not ask for was for him to be God-fearing. Because I knew that I could pray him in. Be very careful what you ask God for because he will give it to you.

Dating In Fear

My landlord and I had been friends for over 12 years he was like a big brother to me I would seek his advice on everything. I trusted him. Once I was separated from my husband, he would say I have a friend that is just right for you. You are a good woman, and you need the right man to take care of you. Your husband is stupid. I was like ok but didn't take him seriously. He would invite me to his parties and events, trying to introduce his friend to me. And I would make up some type of excuse as to why I could not make it. No matter how many times I said no he never stopped asking. One time he had some documents for me to pick up. Normally he would just take them to the car. I noticed about five or six cars in his driveway and none of them was his. I called him to let him know that I was outside. He was like park the car and come in. I was like no I smell a trap. I lied and was like I got a call from the girls I have to go back home right now and did a U-turn. One afternoon I was minding my own business and this voice texted him and told him that you want to meet his friend. So, I was obedient, and I texted him. I also send him the disclaimer to let his friend know in advance that I am Jamaican. Enough send.

My phone rang while I was at my security job, and I thought someone was messing with me. His voice was so soft I thought a woman was calling me. He said no I am Don's friend. We spoke for a few hours he had me laughing the whole time. We made plans to meet up. I said to myself I am going to go into this with a clear mind. I didn't go on Facebook to see what he looks like I didn't even ask for a picture. When I was dating, I had some requirements. I love my men tall dark and handsome and Jamaican. I am a passionate person so most of my conversation topics were very sexual. I am a very sexual person, and I enjoyed a partner that is on my sexual level.

At this point in my life, I had mastered self-care. After leaving my ex-husband I had lost over a hundred pounds; my hair had grown back I was hot shit. Men were approaching me from left to right. I was getting ready to get my mommy makeover surgery mainly a tummy tuck. I had two c-sections. Enough said. I was in love with myself and how I look. I was very proud of the person I had become, and I gave her a new name Lena. Sometimes we must tell ourselves that we are proud of ourselves and what we have accomplished so far in life.

I saw this person coming towards me in the most Haitian shirt in the world. He was averagely built, taller than me, and dark chocolate just as I like my men. But that shirt. I was like please don't let that be him. He sits down and asks me, "Do you like my shirt". I burst out laughing and I almost peed myself. We had a good conversation and he kept me laughing. The next day he texted me and said I will call you after work where I work, I am not allowed to be on my phone but here is my supervisor's number in case of anything they would get hold of him. I was like what. It was just one date. He was not my typical Jamaican man. He was Haitian!!! We don't even speak the same language. He would text me good morning, Beautiful and stuff of that nature and I would look at it but didn't really look at it. I was just looking to have some fun, not for a husband.

Our mutual friend called me and asked so did you guys went out on a date yet and so forth and I was like yes, but I don't know. Don't you know he cussed me out saying His friend was a good man and was tailor-made for me and if I didn't see that he was going to find another woman for him. I was like really.

On date three I asked him what he saw in me. I thought he would mention a body part or even how I look but no. He said I have been praying to God to send me someone like you. I had to sit there for a minute. He said God told him I was going to be his wife. That I would love him how he needs to be loved. I would take care of him unconditionally and that I was beautiful on the outside and the inside. But most of all he could trust me to take care of his heart.

He knew that I had children and he wanted to meet them, but I told him on my terms. Do you think he listened to me? Not at all. He came over one Sunday after church and did a barbeque dinner for me and my girls. He introduced himself to my girls and told them that he and I were dating and that he wanted to get to know them. Then he told them that he worked for Disney and that he could take them any time that they wanted. They started planning which park they wanted to go to first. There he was on the couch sitting between my two girls as if he belonged. Smiles all around. Then this feeling of fear crept up in my stomach and my mind began to race. I was asking myself all kinds of questions, was I doing the right thing? Is he going to hurt my babies? Will he use all my resources, and I have to start all over again? I prayed and asked God to guide me and my feeling. I know that he put Ralph in my life to be my husband so help my fears by removing them. I asked God to build my trust in him. See sometimes bad relationships can cause wounds that we put band-aids over, but they require surgery. Wounds that we don't even realize that we have because we must be strong all the time as single mothers. My fears could have ruined my relationship. I never prayed so much in my life.

Single mothers/parents are the strongest creatures on the earth. There is no manual on how to be a parent. Situations happen and we try our best to fix them with a smile on our faces. Not only are we responsible for protecting and guiding our children but we must plan and take care of the day-to-day responsibilities of running a household. There is no one to turn to and say, "Did you pay the light bill?" We must be very organized and responsible at all times. There is no downtime for us. So, if you want to date a single parent be very serious. We are giving you the little time that we have for ourselves so please don't waste it.

You're not just dating a single parent you're dating their children also, never fall in love with someone before you introduce them to your children that's a receipt for disaster depending on the age of your child. But most importantly divorced single parents are not damaged goods. We were strong enough to step away from a situation that was not healthy for us and our children. God never intended for us to be single parents. The burden of raising a child is not meant for one person. There are days when we don't want to be a parent and are just responsible for ourselves. Parenting is a very hard job, and our children don't make it any easier for us. It could be very draining, and tiresome, you may find yourself crying at times because it can be very overwhelming. We are survivors.

From day one my second oldest daughter Gabby was in love with Ralph, he had become her father. My oldest, not so much. I remember driving to church one Sunday and my girls were arguing quietly. I heard Gabby say I like him. He's going to be great for Mom and us just you see. Jazz was like I don't know. Gabby stops her right there and said he is not only here for Mom but for us too. They became silent and I pretended that I didn't hear anything. From that day on Jazzy changed completely towards Ralph and he became her pop. She loved him so much that she asked him to escort her to her middle school prom and to participate in her graduation.

We went on some dates together and then we went on dates with the children, he always included them. When he came over, he would ask them about the school, their day, and if they needed anything before, he even got to me. I remember the first time he asked to take my girls to go get some ice cream without me. I was like for what. He had lost a bet to the girls, so the reward was ice cream. I tell you I was shitting bricks. My mind went into a negative mode. I don't know if he was a mind reader but. He looked at me and held my face in his hands and said I love you and those girls, and I would never do anything to harm them. Kiss me and was like girls put your shoes on the last one to the car was paying. I took a deep breath and called Jazz on her cell phone. He took the phone and hung up. I was like what. I was beyond pissed. A small voice was like the girls are safe. I tried my best to focus on work. Those were the longest thirty minutes of my life. They come back and I am looking at the girls and they are smiling from ear to ear telling me how they went to get ice cream at the ice cream spot Gabby saw the price and was like let's go to Walmart and get a bucket and some sprinkles. Their prices were too high for just one-time eating. The smile on my girl's face was priceless. I went back to work and listened to them talking while making them create an ice cream sundae. From that day I learned that I could completely be transparent with Ralph. He would see my fears and address them. He never judged me or got angry with me. I began to heal where I was broken.

Allowing Someone Else to Love Me

I kept my relationship with Ralph from everyone. Not that I was ashamed of him but for once in my life, I was really happy on every level. I feared that the moment I shared my relationship with him that my happiness would end. He catered to every aspect of my life, and I was well pleased. I wanted to stay in my little bubble with him and my girls. There were times when our relationship was tested. I remember calling him one day and there was no answer. I was like where is he? He normally calls me when he gets out of work. Hours passed by nothing I must have left about ten messages. Don't judge me, not only was I worried but the girls were as well. Finally, at about midnight, I got a phone call from him. I lost it. I did not give him a chance to explain. I just wanted to be mad. He called me back and was like listen don't say anything. I got out of work early because I wasn't feeling good. I didn't call you because I knew you were sleeping. Yes, I could have texted you but that would have also disturbed you from your sleep. I took some pain medication, and I just woke up. I don't care if you believe me. My bed is not a regular bed. Once I get in it, I go to sleep. I was like what kind of bed do you have? He said you would have to come over to find out. Like a smart ass, I was like I am on my way. Let me tell you something, I did not know a bed could feel like that. He has a California king bed with that extra soft mattress that those athletes sleep on. I got into his bed and all my tension left my body. He went to get me something to drink and by the time he came back, I was knocked out. He let me sleep and woke me up when it was time for him to go to work at 4 am. I was like ok in the future I don't care to text me. I have this policy that when I am sleeping don't wake me up unless the house is on fire. I worked three jobs so when I sleep, I sleep. I am the worst person on this side of the world if you wake me up for something that is not an emergency.

I knew he wanted us to live together but he didn't know how to have that conversation with me. He was at my place every day, he had a key, two bottom drawers, and some closet space. Summertime was approaching and my girls were going to Jamaica for the summer. The day before I left, I told him that whenever he was ready to move in, he didn't have to ask me the answer was yes. Don't you know when I came back in one week, he had completely moved in? All I could do was just laugh.

Living with him was nothing like the prison I felt like when I lived with my ex-husband. We made meals together. He would make that Haitian rice and I would make the meat. We did the house chores together. I would wash and fold and he would put the clothes away. There was never a toilet seat left up. We watched the series together and had actual conversations. He was very playful, considerate, and very affectionate. The girls were not used to that kind of interaction. We had family time, and they loved every minute of it. We sat done and would have a family meeting as if they were a business meeting. He wanted to know everything, and I had no problem showing him everything. I no longer work three jobs but now have two. I was home more with my children. It was very hard for me to leave the house. There is nothing like being in love and feeling, that you are truly loved and valued by someone, and the baby was not afraid to show it.

The combination of our Jamaican/Haitian home was very interesting. I had only dated Jamaican men, so it was easy cooking and taking care of them because we had the same cultural beliefs, and we speak the same language patois. Ralph speaks over seven languages and in his downtime, he listens to his music and shows in his native language Kreole (creole) which we didn't understand. He would teach me and the girls Creole, but my brain was not having it. When I clean, I played my Jamaican music, and we dance while we clean the house. I tried my best to research his culture, national dishes, and things of that nature. I download language apps to learn Creole. By now you can tell I do my research a lot. I am a big respecter of other people's cultures and I try my best to understand and be respectful of their practices and beliefs. I learned that a Haitian party is not just one day they party from Friday night right back to Sunday afternoon. Ralph was a DJ on the side and is great at it. People stay on the dance floor the whole night when he plays. Most of his clients were Haitian and I would go with him. He loves it when I put on a dress with some heels. That would explain why we now have two baby girls under the age of two. I fell in love with him on the dance floor and didn't even know what the words meant but the way he held me and looked straight into my soul was all the explanation that I needed. I spent a lot of time getting to know his friends and family. He would ask me when was he going to me, my friends, and my family. I told him to meet my family and that he would have to take time off from work one Sunday so that he could go to church with me. I thought he would refuse but he was OK.

I could not watch him cook at first. His cooking style was completely different from mine. He uses a lot of fresh seasoning that he would blend together then seasons his meat. Vinegar was also a big ingredient for him. Before he fried anything he would season it then boil it then fry it or bake it. When he made rice, he could fry up his onion and season first then add the rice. He used a lot of oil. Oil was not my best friend. But his food was delicious. When I cook, we season the meat and put it in the fridge to let the season soak into the meat. When we make rice, we use butter. Also, Jamaican food has a flavor that was too spicy for him. So sometimes he would taste and not eat. I had to change how I season the meat, so it wasn't too spicy for him. So, I would try many combinations of seasons. I finally got it I took his fresh seasoning and added my Jamaican seasoning and blend it all together and had him taste it to make sure that it was good for him. Maybe I should bottle it and sell it. He would say I want to taste the food not burn my tongue off. These examples may seem like common sense but these same things can make or break a relationship if we don't take time to know our partner and understand who they are and where they are coming from.

There was a time I would ask him if he was ok. I wanted to make sure that I was taking care of his mental side. He had gone from being responsible for only himself. He had a metro pc and a gang of friends that would cook and tell him to come to pick up his plate. Too now he was the head of a household of 4 people and 2 dogs. His financial obligation had increased by over 150%. Some may say that is what a real man is supposed to do. But I had to make sure that he was never overwhelmed or resentful. He would always say I prayed for the family and that he was ready and ok. He had never been with a woman that cared about him the way I did. I never had to ask for money, he would just give it to me. He would always say I trust you.

Allowing Him to Be the Man in The Relationship

After six months of indescribable happiness, I noticed that $100 was missing every week. I was like what is he doing? The old feeling crept in, and I was like is he cheating and giving money to another chick? I prayed and asked God to guild me because here was this man that spent all his time with me and my girls. I know where he was at any given point of the day so what was up? I refuse to go thru his phone, check his pockets, or anything crazy like that I was just going to ask him. So, when he came home, I let him relax first and then I was like a baby I notice money missing every week. He was yes, I sent it to the number's lady. I am like what lady? For my islanders, some call it partner, susu, Haitians call it numbers. It started where his hand was $2500 a draw to now three years later his hand is over $10,000. This was his way of saving money and paying down big debts. With his method of saving money. I was able to go down to one job and build up our savings. We paid off vehicles and eliminated debt in record time.

My friends were concerned because they had not heard from me. I didn't want to tell them I was in a relationship because they would rub it in my face. But I finally told them, and they were happy for me to meet him. He wasn't the typical man that I had dated in the past and I was a little bit nervous. They each met him on separate occasions, and they all said the same thing if you love him, we love him. For my saved friends it was when you bring him to church. I never hid my spiritual side from him. He would hear me pray and speak in my heavenly language. When he did meet my saved friends, the conversation was a bit on the when are you guys getting married side.

When he introduced me to his friends it was my wife. They would compliment me on how beautiful I was and how happy he was. I would see them in the neighborhood and would say hi to Ralph's wife. Marriage again was another big fear for me. I had to move to another state to get my divorce from my first husband. We were married in New York and lived in Florida. When you want to get a divorce, you have to follow both states' guidelines. New York said you had to be separated for one year before they considered granting a divorce. The state of Florida was like I could not deny him access to my home. So, I gave up my home, moved into a hotel with my girls, and then rented a place under my friend's name. Then he found out where we were so I had to move to New York where I knew my ex would not follow me. We had no property together, but I gave him my big boy (F150). The divorce process was not easy. I was glad when they awarded custody of my girls to me and that he had to pay child support.

I was raised that you are only supposed to live with your husband I was happy living with Ralph without thinking of marriage. At the beginning of our relationship, I told Ralph that I didn't want to get married again because of what I went through with my first husband. The word marriage would just make me angry and upset and I would hear those prison doors closing behind me in my head. I guess it was because secretly if my relations did not work out all I had to do was pack my things and leave. But to leave a marriage is not so easy. I like the fact that I could just leave without having to separate anything or get the government involved. Not that I was planning on leaving Ralph because he was everything that I asked for and more. My girls had already told me that if Ralph and I broke up that they were going with him.

Like with dating marriage began to haunt me. I would make doctor's appointments for Ralph, and they would ask are you, his wife. When we had our first daughter together and I was trying to help him with his paperwork since we were not married, he had to take FMLA unpaid because I was not his wife. The company he works for has amazing family benefits but guess what, I had to be his legal wife. And the list goes on. I didn't have to pray on this one because I know that we must get married. God has a funny way of reminding you of what you are supposed to be doing. The voice came to me if you think you are happy now marriage unlock certain blessing. Although we were good people and Ralph was going to church with me it was not enough.

One day Ralph came to me and said to me you know one day we are going to get m. and he changed it to a commitment ceremony, and I just smiled. He wants us to get married in Hawaii because he said that is what I deserve. He starts talking about whom we are going to invite straight down to the decorations. All I could do was just hug him and kiss him until I started crying. See at church they have activities for marriage and seriously dating couples and he is like I want to go to all the events. I was just so happy that he wanted to spend time with my church family that I didn't see how much I was healing. One day Ralph came home from work, and he was limping. I told him to take a hot shower so I could give him a massage. I rubbed his back and legs then he was like my feet hurt baby. Now, this is when I realized that I loved this man. If you know me, I Hate feet. Don't put them on me or wiggle your toes in front of me. But I got some oil, and I rubbed that man's feet even in between his toes. I rubbed his feet so good he fell asleep. As I was rubbing his feet the years of hurt and pain began to strip away. I was no longer afraid to love again, I felt that I could be completely transparent with him. At that moment I realized that I wanted to be Ralph's wife. That I wanted to wake up to him every morning and if I wasn't in my late 30s, I would have given him a baseball team full of babies.

I was able to heal from the pain and hurt that I experienced in my first marriage. By allowing Ralph to love me and by showing him all of me flawed and all. He took every step with me during my healing process. But most of all I prayed, and I trust God even when my flesh was weak, and I wanted to return to when it was just me and my girls. Where I felt safe. If didn't trust again I would not have this wonderful man that loves me and our 2 beautiful daughters together. Not only did I heal but my two older daughters experience what it was like to have a father in their life every day. Taking them to school and doctor's appointments. Spending quality time with them. He has taught them what the role of a man is supposed to be in a relationship. He has shown them how a healthy relationship between a man and a woman is supposed to look. I no longer have to worry about them when they start dating if they are going to make the same mistakes that I made. My babies are safe from that.

Resistance

Sam Moore

The path of most resistance.

When you become the decision and not the choice.

Where you discover more trees than tread.

The path of most resistance.

Where you sow your seeds with tears.

Surviving seasons of barren branches.

The path of most resistance.

Where correction is not coercion,

And grace abounds.

The path of most resistance.

Feeling the warmth of the sun on your face,

The wind at your back.

The path of most resistance.

Where you find purpose.

Where you find yourself.

Strengthened.

Conscious.

Renewed.

Parental Remorse

Jessica Newman

Dear Gem,

I see you looking down and frustrated what is it that's troubling you.? Baby, you need to let it out and get it off your chest.

Don't hold it in this is a safe place. Take your time, you can trust me. Is it what I think it is???? Listen, you won't be the first or the last. I understand how you are feeling I felt the same way when it happened to me. I was 19 lost confused and basically, just living in search of being loved and then I thought I finally found true love, real love, everlasting love. The love that little girls dream of. Or so I believed. I just knew that having my baby was going to fill the void I had in my life for so long. But Gem let me tell you something that I said in my head but never out loud. You will be the first to know my dirty little secret. This one thing that has been eating me alive since the very first day, I'm just going to have to say there is no way around it. Once it's out it's out. I won't be able to take it back and some may look at me with disgust but I'm hoping some will understand and have empathy or at least tell me to.

I didn't want to be a mother back then and sometimes even to this day, I question whether I should have aborted my first child and gone on with my life. I can't believe I said it. Now don't sit there looking at me with wide eyes. It needed to be said. I finally stood in my truth that motherhood was not for me. Abortion was such a taboo word when I was growing up. I heard about it but most of the time I was faced with "you are going to go to hell if you kill your baby." God will never forgive you. You are going to die on the table. The babies you kill will haunt you forever. So instead of dealing with burning in hell for eternity and never being loved by God, I choose to take the path that looked good for everyone else but left me bewildered and distraught.

There are many women whose only dream is to have a child. Some struggle just to be able to conceive. So, I can understand if some people will call me selfish or ungrateful as I sit here with 4 healthy children that took little to no effort to conceive. But to be honest I think I just wanted to be a mother because that's what everyone said I was supposed to become. Eventually one day little girls grow up to be mothers. No one ever asked me if that's what I wanted. They just said "you are going to be a great mom just like your mom" and hear I stand almost 20 years later after having my first child and still struggle over the fact that I never wanted to be a mother. I never really put a lot of thought into what my life would have been like without kids. I can only assume that I would have a lot of time to myself and money. Life may have been stress-free. Maybe I would have fulfilled my dream of becoming a doctor. Or my life could have been empty and longing for something to fill the many voids in my life. At this point, all I can do is assume and try not to focus on the "what ifs." Don't get me wrong, I love my kids, and I will do any and everything for them but if I had a choice a long time ago, I can't say 100% that I would have chosen this path for my life. Please God don't hate me. But for me to heal I need to be honest. It is necessary for me to look this situation dead in the eye and confront it. I need to finally free myself from it. My relationships with my children have been affected long enough. The turmoil, discomfort, heartaches, and pain I have caused from the continuous denial of my true feelings, no longer serve a purpose in my life. Sometimes I did my best to try to hide it but at times it was written all over my face. Gem sit back and let me really explain my remorse.

Where it all started, I guess the best place to start with my troubling path to motherhood would be with my firstborn. Your first child is always like an "experiment" I had no real guidance. I just remember doing what I thought was right. It was love at first sight. I lay on the hospital bed pushing and screaming and as soon as she entered the world I began crying. The old folks used to always say you cry when a child is born because you don't know what life they are going to have and you rejoice when someone dies because you know what kind of life they have lived, and where they are going. Who knew that those tears I shed that day would not be the only tears I would shed for the next 19 years?

In life, everyone can be a part of the same situation but have a different viewpoint. That is how I would describe my relationship with my firstborn. In my eyes, I gave her my best. I loved her, took care of her, and thought that I was showing her a good example of what it meant to work hard and take care of your children. Of course, her version of life is the complete opposite. Is she wrong? Yes and No. Did I provide for her yes, did she get everything her heart desired? No. Was I able to provide her stability, yes? Was it what she needed or longed for, nope! I can go on and on and back and forth about all the things that she thought I didn't give her but I know in my heart that I felt like I was giving her all that I had.

I will be honest I was not the most affectionate mother back then and I still to this day struggle with showing and receiving affection. I believe it all began when I was a child and the type of relationship I had with my own mother. Yes, I knew my mother loved and cared about me, but was she constantly hugging me and every moment telling me that she loved me, no. I knew that it was nothing that this woman would not have done for me. She would give her last to make sure I had all that I needed. That is how she showed her love. I didn't need to hear every day "I love you "or that you mean so much to me. I knew that there was nothing that could break the bond that my mother and I had so I took that same mentality with my own children as long as I'm doing for you and showing you, why do I need to say it repeatedly? The struggles and sacrifices I made should have been more than enough to prove my love. Well, not for my firstborn. She's more of a hug-me-tell-me kind of person not just give me show me or do for me. She needed to hear it constantly over and over and I couldn't give her that because that made me uncomfortable. Sometimes just the thought of expressing my love to my children made my stomach turn into knots. I would cringe at the fact that I had to hug them.

Does that make me a bad person? Or does that make me a person who struggled with my own self-love? At nineteen I really didn't love myself so how could I give my child something that I didn't even have within me? I had to fake it. I would put on a phony smile and pretend that I had it all together. I portrayed myself as a mother who loved her kids unconditionally without ever second-guessing myself. That is what everyone wants you to believe but that is not my truth. My truth is I constantly questioned my love for my children, I constantly questioned if I were good enough to be their mother. Was I making all the right decisions? Did I make a mistake by choosing them over me? As time passed on with my firstborn, I thought eventually she would just succumb to my way of doing things and that she will get used to me not being affectionate and then just rely on knowing that eating, having a roof over her head, and clothes on her back were good enough.

She was constantly seeking my affection and I did not know how to give it to her. We struggled, we battled, and we bumped heads. I was in denial and overlooked a lot of things. in the beginning, I thought she seems OK. She should be all right and then as time went on, I noticed that we began to grow further apart. Our conversations when she was age 10 were easy and non-confrontational. Then out of nowhere, this teenager appeared in front of me who was defiant, troublesome, and disconnected. I didn't know how to handle it. My baby, my firstborn stood in front of me lost and confused and I could not help her. I needed help myself and was unsure of which direction to go in. Deep down I hated the relationship I had with her, but I also blamed her. She went outside and found someone else to give her that love and affection. Instead of looking at it as a cry for help, I took it as a stab in my back.

The guilt and pain I felt during these troubling years, reminded me of the feelings I had after losing my mother. Here I was trying to be a great mother but still was not fully healed from losing my own mother. I prayed and asked God to help me with my child. The blame game was so deep I began to overlook her defiant behavior. She was constantly hurting me and hindering our relationship. At one point I questioned if we could ever really have a true mother-daughter relationship. The rollercoaster rides of events that we experienced over the years were difficult, but they stretched and shaped both of us. Now our relationship isn't perfect, but we have learned how to communicate and learn each other's love language. At times I still question myself when it comes to her, but I do believe that time and an intentional effort on both our parts will one day help create a bond that can withstand any adversaries. A bond that I longed for with my own mother.

Second in Line

Now you would have thought that after all the doubt, worry, fear, and insecurities I had felt with my firstborn that I would not even dream of having any more children. Wrong! Not even a full two years later after my first, I was pregnant again with my second child. Once again, I had to make the decision of whether I was going to keep my child. I was 21, in my last year of college. Still trying to navigate life and motherhood. I was determined to finish school and provide a

stable environment for my child. When I found out I was pregnant, I was in denial.

My belly began to grow quickly, and I still wasn't sure if I really wanted or was ready to be a mother of two. I know you may be thinking, why didn't I get on birth control if I was not sure about motherhood? The truth is I was on birth control but being young, inconsistent, and still a little naive, I didn't think I would get pregnant again so quickly. My boyfriend (baby daddy) now husband, at the time, did not want another child. Later on, I would find out that he had another woman pregnant at the same time as me, but that story is for another day. He begged me repeatedly to have an abortion and I finally agreed. The first time we drove up to the abortion clinic, there were protestors standing outside. I told him to leave, and we could try again another day. The next time I went I did not have the courage to walk in. It wasn't until the third time, I said today is the day I am going to walk in here and have an abortion. I sat in the waiting room until the nurse called me to the back. I laid on the bed and watched as the nurse put the ultrasound on my stomach. I was afraid to look at the screen. As I stared at the ceiling, I anticipated what she would say. To my surprise, I was told I was unable to have an abortion. So here I was about to face another obstacle in my life.

The day I went into labor was full of twists and turns. I was sitting in class when my contractions began. I knew something wasn't right. No matter what I tried to do I could not get comfortable. I decided to drive myself with my 2yr old in the back seat to the ER. I walked into the ER and told the doctors "I think my water broke" They ran all the typical tests and said, "You are about to have this baby, you are already 3cm dilated." The fear that came over me in that instant was overwhelming. I couldn't believe I was about to have another baby and she was coming early. I thought of all the things that could go wrong. I was alone and terrified. I trusted the doctors would make the best decision and I prayed that God would allow her to overcome any obstacles she may have faced due to her being premature.

Everything happened so quickly. My best friend came and picked up my oldest. My baby daddy unbeknownst to me was already at another hospital visiting his new daughter. A few of my classmates came to the hospital to keep me company until he was able to make it. At 5 o'clock the next morning, my baby girl was born via emergency C-section weighing 4 lbs. Was I ready to potentially have a child who may have health issues? Definitely not. Was I up for the challenge? No, but I knew I had no choice. After nine days in the NICU, my baby was strong enough to

go home, and just two weeks after having her I was right back at school focused and determined not to become a statistic. Two babies under two, senior in college, a cheating baby daddy, and no family support. At this point, I truly thought I was going to lose my mind. I took my doubt and fears and turn them into my desire to succeed.

My relationship with my second child was the opposite of my oldest. My second daughter was mild-tempered, easy to get along with, and always did what she was told. I cannot recall a time when I had to yell, discipline, or punish her for any inappropriate behaviors. She had few friends, worked hard in school, and always helped around the house. I thought finally I have a child who loves and respects me. I needed her more than she needed me. I put so many responsibilities on her, and even though she was the youngest at the time, I knew I could depend on her. I felt that God gave me a child whom I did not have to worry about because he knew how difficult my life was at the time. But once again the self-doubt and insecurities crept right back into our mother-daughter relationship. I have lost track of the number of times I have gone to my second born and cried and looked for acceptance and reassurance from her. I wanted her to love me the way I desired my oldest child to love me. Once I felt that real unconditional love from her, I never wanted to lose it. I put all my hopes in dreams into her. She was going to be the one who saved me, who would take care of me. She was going to be the one who helped me. While my oldest was being wild and reckless she was home cleaning, cooking, and looking after the little ones (I had two more children after her). As she became a teenager and it reached the time for her to leave and go to college, I put so much guilt on her that I convinced her it was best that she stayed home and went to a local community college. I couldn't bear losing the one child who truly loved me. But my child was hurting and frustrated and I didn't see it or I did not want to see it. I just assumed she had a better handle on life than most kids her age. I never really asked her was the burden too much to carry.

Until I noticed our relationship began to change. She wanted freedom and she wanted her older sister to be held accountable for all the pain and anguish she had caused. Not just to me, but to everyone in the family. My second child was hurting, and I didn't even know how to comfort her. I remember when she had her first real break up and she was crying, any other person with some type of emotions would have hugged their child and tried to make them feel better. I just gave her some advice and told her to move on there are other fish in the sea. Why couldn't I show emotions? Why was I so afraid to let my guard down? My children needed me to be sympathetic, caring, and nurturing. I just wanted them to do right, keep my house clean and stay out of the way. My thought process was crazy and misconstrued but this is the way I was feeling for a long time. Around the age of thirty, I realized that many of my issues came from anxiety. My constant worrying was turning me into an on-edge person with unstable emotions. I was constantly yelling, taking my aggression out on my children (not physically) but mentally I was detached from them. I worked, came home, took care of the house, fed them, and went to bed. This was my life for many years. Disconnected, emotionally detached, and looking for love.

The constant worry of being able to provide for them became more than I could bare. I was there but not there. I was looking for a way out but was not sure which way to go. I was depressed and longing for some stability in my life. I tried so hard to be a good mother to my girls but I felt like I was constantly failing. I began to have thoughts of suicide but then I realized that I couldn't leave my children. They needed me just as much as I needed them. I fought to change the way I was feeling and I realized the only one who could help me was God. I decided in 2010 that it

was time that I found myself a good church home and try to change my life not just for me but for my children. My relationship with my second child wavered a little but it never diminished. Still to this day, as she works and goes to school, her family is always her priority. We are much closer now and she can come and talk to me about anything. She makes me want to show and express my love and affection more and more each day. I don't even know if she knows how much she has impacted my life.

Third Times A Charm

My one and only son came into this world abruptly. I finished college working at a daycare center and trying to get my life on the right track. At the time the girls were five and three. I didn't think I was ready for another one, but my baby daddy and I were in a somewhat good space and by this time he had five girls already and really wanted a boy. Not that I had any magic tricks or potions that would guarantee a boy, but I felt in my heart that this time around he would finally get his boy and then I would be his only baby mother that had his son. I know my thought process was a hot mess but even at 26 years of age, I still didn't value and respect myself. I was so excited to finally find out that I was having a boy. I couldn't wait to rush home and let my baby daddy know that he will finally have someone to carry on his name. My son was a force to be reckoned with. From the time he was able to walk, he was always getting himself into trouble. Once he started school that was the beginning of my constant headache. He was difficult to handle at times and not having his father in the home consistently did not help. I had to deal with the constant phone calls from teachers complaining about his lack of focus and disruptive behavior. I blamed myself because even though he had a father, I had decided to move myself and my children hundreds of miles away from their dad so that I could have some peace of mind in my life. My son struggled immensely. It was so bad I decided to let him repeat kindergarten because he did not learn anything.

I knew it was more than just behavior issues he was struggling with. I did some research and decided to get him tested for ADHD. Not to my surprise at age 6 he was diagnosed with ADHD and opposition defiance disorder. I struggled with excepting that something was wrong with my son. I blamed myself, I blamed his dad and I felt once again I failed as a mother. There were many days I would sit in my car and just cry because I did not know what to do. I prayed that one day he would just grow out of it and be a normal kid. Even though I knew in my heart he was a normal kid, I just couldn't understand why he had to struggle so much in school. It wasn't until a few years after his diagnosis that I learned that his father exhibited these same behaviors and struggles in school. I thought I was fighting hard enough for my son to succeed and get through this. I tried medication, changing his diet, and getting tutors but nothing worked. I also have to be honest and say I was not very consistent with anything I tried. I was overwhelmed with taking care of three kids, working, and trying to keep a relationship together that was falling apart right in front of me. My priorities at the time were not in the right place. I wanted to help him more, but sometimes I didn't have the energy to fight so I just gave in. If he misbehaved, I would threaten to punish or spank him but as soon as we got home he would watch tv play video games and terrorize his older sisters.

Nothing was working. I wanted to walk away and come back when my kids got their life together. But I was their mother and once again they needed my emotional support. I finally decided to face the truth about my son and instead of blaming myself, I decided to fight for him and become his advocate. I went to meetings, found alternative ways to help deal with his ADHD, and provided the love and support he needed. Yes, I made mistakes along the way, but I was determined to help him succeed. This was not an easy task and still to this day my son struggles but he knows he has my support and that I will always have his back. I resented my son for a long time. I thought God was punishing me because in the beginning I only wanted a son so I could have something to brag about to the other baby mommas. I also wanted a son because I thought he was going to fix the brokenness in my relationship with his father. There was no way his dad could leave me after having his one and only son. Once I shifted my focus back on my son and not the external distractions, I knew I wasn't being punished but that God knew I was capable and strong enough to help my son. They always say God doesn't give you more than you can bear. Clearly, God thinks I am as strong as an ox.

My son has always been loving and affectionate. Not sure where it came from or why, but he never had a problem with showing his emotions. He constantly gives hugs and says I love you. I was uncomfortable with my son showing so many emotions. I did not want him to be labeled as soft or a punk. I would constantly tell him to stop crying or toughen up. I would let my fear and anxiety get the best of me. I was constantly worrying about my son's sexual orientation. Even though he never showed me any signs that he was confused about who he was or whom he

liked, I just didn't want to have to deal with anything else that could have been a hindrance in his life. I prayed that he would grow up to like girls. I did not want him to have to deal with any other issues in addition to his ADHD. Let's be clear I do not have any issues with the LGBTQ community, I just didn't want that for my son. That was one thing I did not have to worry about. He is like his father in more ways than one.

After the third child, I was still struggling with my own self-love and expressing my love. This desire my children had to constantly receive love was overwhelming at times. I thought once again my struggles and sacrifice were enough. But they were constantly pushing me out of my comfort zone and trying to make me love them the way that they needed to be loved. I. Just wanted to be a good mom but still didn't quite understand this motherly role. I followed many trends and jumped on different bandwagons when it came to being a mother. I took good advice and some bad advice. Through trial and error, I somewhat figured out what I thought was best for my children.

My son is a respectable, handsome, intelligent young man. I want to believe that even though I wasn't always there for him emotionally, I know I have shaped him into the young man he is striving to become. I truly love the relationship that I have with him. He talks to me about girls, his frustrations with school, and even when he is having difficulties with his friends. I pray as he gets older that he will always know how much I love and appreciate him. Despite my shortcomings, my goal each day is to continue to strive to be the mother that all my children need.

Four And Done

The last of the Mohicans. My little princess arrived when I was in a different mind space. I was going to church, figuring out how to love myself, and learning how to set boundaries in my relationships. I struggled for many years with loving myself. Even though in 2014 I wasn't completely standing in my truth, I did know what I wanted and needed more in life. My children were 11, 9, and 5 when I gave birth to my last baby girl. I was 31 working as a pre-k teacher, married, and living in a nice house in the suburbs. I thought for sure things were really beginning to fall into place.

When the last of the Mohicans stepped on the scene once again I was faced with my troublesome mothering abilities. After her adventurous entrance into this world (almost in Walmart), I had to learn to navigate life with four children. Clearly, I still did not learn my lesson, but I guess I was trying to get it right. People always say the last child gets away with murder, and I am here to tell you my little one took a bite out of crime. Between work, going back to school, being a wife, and trying to have a life, I could not balance it all. It was a constant struggle to meet everyone's needs. I relied heavily on my two oldest girls to help with the baby and around the house. I was hanging on by a thread and drowning in my silent sorrows.

Finally, one thing I did after having my last child was to make sure I would not have anymore. I made the decision to tie my tubes. There was no way I was going to mess up any more kids mentally. But seriously, having a baby in your 30s is way different from having a baby in your 20s.

She grew up so fast right in front of my eyes. She was rotten (still is to this day). I didn't establish any boundaries with her. I allowed her to do what she wanted and thought that every little sassy thing she said or did was cute. Boy, was I wrong for allowing this type of behavior? You live and you learn. I just wanted her to grow up quickly so I could finally be free and live my life. Remember I have been a mother since the age of 20 and never really lived my life. I thought finally it was time for me. With my fourth child, I never thought about not keeping her. By this time of my life, I truly understood what abortion was and the negative effects it can have on your life. I no longer felt like I couldn't have a life with a fourth baby, I just needed to figure out how to balance my life. Balance is the key word. Something I continue to struggle with every day of my life. Now that I am older being consistent is the key to success. I don't have time for laziness, disorder, or inconsistencies.

My baby keeps me on my toes. She is smart well beyond her years. She forces me to have mother-daughter time with her. It is a weekly requirement that we spend quality time together doing something she likes, and she does not take no for an answer. She makes sure I go to church, and she stays on me about staying on task and keeping my obligations. She won't let me slip back into my old ways of mothering. She has high expectations and wants me to meet these goals daily. I love how she loves me. I think it was something that I was searching for a needed for a very long time. She makes me want to be a better mother and never disappoint her. Even though I know I can't give her all her heart desires, I do know that my effort, love, and support are all she really needs. I Thank God that he allowed me to have one more so that I could really see that I am not such a bad mother after all.

Always A Bonus

The love I have for my bonus daughter is truly amazing. Even though my husband has three other children, his first daughter holds a special place in my heart. I have been in her life since she was almost two years old. I was in college the first time I met her. She gravitated to me so easily. I wanted to make a good impression on her so that her daddy would like me more (my thought process was terrible, lord forgive me). I wanted her to know I was a good person. At two I really don't think she cared who I was just if I could give her all the snacks she wanted. As time went on, we didn't have much of a relationship. It wasn't until she was 15 that she came to live with us. I was all for her living with us but I did worry about how she would feel being around me on a daily basis. Truth is back then I believed that my husband's other children felt some kind of way about me. I thought they felt as if I took their dad away from them. Even though that wasn't the truth I can see how children could perceive me as being in the way of their relationship.

So here I was with four children in a three-bedroom apartment and here comes another child for me to love and care for. This time it was different. She wasn't my biological child, so she didn't have to truly love or like me. I was once told the deepest expression of love is to love a child that is not your own. That is all I wanted to give her, was my love and adoration. But of course, I failed miserably. I responded out of guilt at first instead of just focusing on loving her, I was trying to please her and force her to like me. I overlooked a lot of her attitude or her inability to love me like she was really my daughter. I had too many expectations and wasn't giving her the grace and time, she needed to adapt to her new environment. I just thought it was going to happen naturally and quickly. I was impatient and disregarded her feelings time and time again. Despite my inability to meet her needs at the beginning of our relationship, she did like me and loved being a part of our family. That doesn't mean we did not have our share of issues. Of course, at

15 you already are set in your ways and once I got past the guilt I had to learn to deal with the difficult behaviors. Not that there were many, but I did feel like I had to set boundaries in order not to feel like I was walking around my house on eggshells.

It took time for us to learn from each other and love each other in a respectable way. Trust me I made many mistakes, but I held myself accountable and knew how to ask for forgiveness and accept her for who she was. I also recognized that all the issues we faced were not just because of me but of some personal things she had to learn to deal with. Counseling was our go and it made a huge difference in our relationship. As time went on our bond grew stronger. I still remember the first day she called me Mom. I couldn't believe it. I didn't know if I should say something or just answer her. I decided in an instant to just go with the flow and answer her. It filled my heart with joy to know that you considered me a motherly figure in her life. We faced many bumps and hurdles along the way, but as time went on and we both matured and learn how to respect each other it created a bond that could never be broken. She is my bug-a-boo still to this day, but I would not change her for anything in this world. The relationship I have with my bonus daughter is the same relationship I desire and continue to strive for with my firstborn. If you were to ask my bonus daughter today if was I perfect, she would definitely say no but if you asked her if I do my best and loved her with my whole heart, I would have to believe she would say yes without a doubt in her mind.

Choices

Gem, in life we are all faced with choices. Good or bad, wrong or right we had to make choices that may impact us for a day, a month, a year, or the rest of our lives. I can't help to sometimes think back to that day as a 19 yr old and having to decide did I want to have a baby with a man I hardly knew, and raise a child even though I was still a child myself. That one choice catapulted my life in a direction that I was not prepared for but gave me strength and courage that I continue to carry inside of me today. The feeling of regret towards choosing to become a mother is a difficult feeling that I had to face. Why regret? For a long time, I believed that I was not good enough to be my children's mother. I believed they needed someone better than me. I regretted not giving them the life that they truly deserved. A life that resembled my upbringing. They deserved a great life and I just never truly believed that I was capable of giving them that. Once I finally realized that their lives did not turn out so badly, I no longer carry the regret. Now I carry the lessons and the wisdom that I obtained over the years. I want other women to know that it is okay to not desire to be a mom. It doesn't make you less of a woman. And mothers who are struggling to be a mother, the fact that you get up every day and try your best is all that really matters. Making the choice to be a mother was more than just deciding to keep my children. Being a mother meant that I took on the responsibility to raise them to become respectful, productive citizens in this world.

I was given the responsibility to raise children who knew their purpose and knew their position in life. I was gifted the responsibility to nurture and love someone that no matter what I did or thought I didn't do, would love me unconditionally. All this time I thought I was making a decision for their lives but in actuality, I was making a decision for my life. God knew exactly what I needed and each one of my children had molded me into the strong, courageous, force-to-be-reckoned-with you see here today.

Gem as I sit here across from you, you may feel hurt, pain, and frustration but what you can't see is the triumph, the victory, the glory on the other side of your choice. Choose wisely, choose deeply, and choose what is best for you. Don't let anyone or anything influence what is best for you. Pray, meditate, and pray again until you can hear God clearly. If every time in life we would go to God before making a choice, we would live life with fewer regrets and fewer uncertainties.

From the time we are born, God has already created a path for our life. Your choices in life determine if the paths will have rocks, gravel, hills, and valleys to climb. Just know that whatever you decide, God is the only person you must answer to. Make your choice and stand in your truth.

All Life

Sam Moore

I used to view love as a novelty item. Something that I had to win, to earn like a carnival prize.

People would love me, and then leave me.

Take my loyalty for granted, taking my love for granted. Yet still, I stayed, because the allegiance always reigned stronger than the abuse.

I never felt like a "long-time" love.

My eyes peeled. The fog began to dissipate. I started to "see men as trees", and my vision became clearer and clearer. My aptitude to stay in places that no longer served me became an antagonizing thorn in my side. Something that I could no longer ignore or set aside. I developed a new standard.

Time. Time alone allowed me to create time for mindful living. Healing, living life, creating my own experiences, and creating space.

Then, love came. It came from myself first, as it always should have. I loved myself deeper than I ever had, deeper than anyone had. Then, you came.

Love like yours feels like mountain fresh air. I can breathe. I can breathe deeply. I no longer had to win love, it was given to me like an award, like a Nobel Peace Prize.

It is rich, velvety, and warm. Safe and sound. Strong, yet gentle. Full of accountability and grace. Pushing me while tandemly holding me close. A corrective experience that has already proven to break generational curses.

I used to be told that I loved love, and that might be true, but now, I see that love, loves me too.

Now I See Me...Now You Don't

Mel V

Growing up my life wasn't easy.

Broken home

Feeling alone

No one ever heard me.

Unbearably invisible to those closest to me

Never understanding the struggle

Broken girls grow into damaged women.

Empty voids of nothingness

Lost in her own shadow.

Quietly she drifted away.

Leaving nothing but a trail

Too bad no one noticed.

Her reflection still the same

Freedom has finally found her

Not a care left in the world

Broken girl now damaged woman

Blossomed into a queen.

Dear Gem,

So, I need you to do me a favor, get up and go stand in front of your mirror, or if you really don't feel like it grabs your compact mirror out of your purse and open it. Take a long hard look at the person staring back at you. Now ask yourself, do you recognize that person? Do you like that person? Do you love that person? It's OK, be honest with yourself because I'm about to get real honest. I write this letter to you three months away from my 40th birthday and would it shock you to know that not too long ago my answer to all of those questions would've been yes. Well, at least not truthfully. If someone would've asked me those questions, the words that came out of my mouth would've absolutely been yes but in the back of my mind, I would've been telling myself why are you lying? And the truth of the matter is although currently on most days I can confidently say yes, there are still some days if I'm honest, the answer would still be no. But you know what? that's OK! Because one of the biggest steps in growth and transparency is first, to be honest with yourself.

So, let's take a journey! Let me share with you how someone can lose their identity, well actually, never really have one, be completely oblivious that it's lost, appear fully functional, and live like this for over 30 years. A living, breathing, walking ghost. Yes, you heard me a right ghost! There is a body completely invisible to everyone, even herself.

Lil Ole Miss Who?

My childhood was very confusing. I lived two very different types of lives. I was loved, belittled,

encouraged, abused, and at the same time made to feel worthy and worthless at the same time. To start off, I had two parents who seemingly, for lack of better words, couldn't stand each other. Sometimes, I wondered how they lasted long enough to even create me. My mother hated that I looked like my dad or at least I did then. She hated that I loved him and did everything possible to destroy that. At a very early age, she made it a point to tell me that when she was pregnant, he didn't want me and that he wanted her to have an abortion. I know right! Pretty messed up to tell your kid. So, starting from there my idea of self and my level of worthiness were already up for question. How could somebody not want you before you even got here? You don't even know me yet! Then to make matters worse, when I was six, she forced me to move with her and leave everything that I had come to know, and to the point, I made above, my dad just let me. Now comes the question, does he or did he really not want me? Why is he so easy to let me go? No fight or at least not that I could see. All this put me in a position to be the target of ridicule as I grew up. Every characteristic of me that was like my dad was a trigger for my mom and vice versa. It was a constant battle of whom I should or shouldn't be.

Then input my stepfather 's daughter. She came to live with us and let's just say my life went from bad to worse. I became the blame for everything. I got beaten even if I did nothing wrong.

It was their word against mine and unfortunately, my mother, who I assumed would have been on my side, believed them without fail. So, there are now three against one. Not fair, would you say?

I was constantly compared to my stepsister. Remember, at the beginning of this journey, we

talked about the issues with questioning my worth? Major Factor!!

As a kid I was chubby. We're going to jump into that a little later but imagine being taken shopping and being left out or told you can only get a few things because they can't find stuff to

fit you. Or maybe no man is going to want you or find you attractive if you don't look a certain

way. Yeah, really racking up the worth points! Without any real true value or self-worth and just being plain tired, I stopped caring. So, I rebelled. I was out in the streets, gangbanging and

being reckless, skipping school, from straight A's to almost flunking out. Wait, did I forget to

mention how at the age of 12 I was molested at my nephew's birthday party and instead of being comforted by my mother I got beaten and was told that it was my fault, I shouldn't have been where I was. Well, maybe that's all men would want for me and that imagery and those feelings filled my head for the next 20 years.

So somewhere around fifteen, I decided to move back with my dad. I guess you could say things.

were good for the most part. He did his best to be a good parent. He had his moments and flaws.

It's funny because when you're dealing with stuff in life and you're walking around with this constant looming question mark, all of the great things can so very easily be out shadowed by the small moments. I remember one day, and I guess this was my dad trying to encourage me to lose weight, he said to me "no man will find you attractive. You're not appealing to the eye and it's all about the visual or men". Then I remember once when I was in college, yes this is from someone who I just said had almost flunked out not too long ago, I got it together, and got into college, premed major nonetheless. Well anyway, I remember it was the hardest semester ever and I got five A's, one B, and a D. He berated me for that D without any acknowledgment of the five A's and B. Still not good enough!

Then let's add growing up with issues of being multi-racial. People have this idea of what you should and shouldn't look like. So, I wasn't black enough, I wasn't Jamaican enough, I wasn't Spanish enough, my nose is too straight, my hair was too curly, and my eyes were too light. It was always something to set off this feeling of unworthiness, but not enough. So, imagine this being your life from childhood, most of your teenage life, and then into adulthood. But let's just focus on the early years right now. The formidable years are when things are supposed to be set in a place where your mentality and your mindset about yourself are supposed to be formulated.

Imagine if everywhere you went and everywhere you turned, in everything that happened to you, you were made to feel like you weren't enough. Constantly competing, constantly feeling like you were overlooked, constantly feeling like they wish you were somebody else, and this is how the saga began.

The Weight of The Weight

As I mentioned earlier, I was kind of a chubby kid. In society, we often find it funny to joke about little chubby kids but imagine for much of your life being called fatso, dumpling, fatty, fatty boom boom, chunky, roly-poly, and the list can go on and on. Even when it's supposedly being said as a joke with cute little nicknames these things leave lasting impressions in your mind of who you are and in your worth. If you are doing this to overweight people in your life, STOP IT!!! Often times people think that doing this, it'll trigger some sort of reverse reaction in you to lose weight or to choose to view yourself differently, and for most people, it does the exact opposite. I didn't necessarily grow up and get smaller, I grew up and I got bigger.

Always hearing in the back of my mind fat so, fatty, dumpling, chunky, fatty boom boom. So every time I walked out of my house, or I turned on the TV, nobody looked like me, and the people that did look like me were not favored, they were not desired, and they were not considered beautiful. You're almost taught to feel like you were considered someone who got the leftovers or the scraps and so that's how life was for me. For any guy that did approach me or wanted to talk to me, my initial assumption was he only wants one thing, so I gave it to him and waited for him to go on his way. Unfortunately, most men that came into my life proved me right.

Gems, have you ever questioned your worth solely based on your sexual appearance or your sexual desire? Or wondered if all you are is the little hot spot, a little wet box? That's all you had to offer. Well, that was me. From high school to college to young adulthood, in and out of pointless relationships but always felt like the only thing that a male wanted for me was what was between my legs.

Earlier when I mentioned that I was twelve years old when I got molested, all it did was fortify thoughts that had been long implanted. In the back of my mind, all I kept thinking was that all men see when they looked at me was sex. They didn't see beauty, they didn't see strength, they didn't see smarts, they just saw somewhere to get their nut off and keep it going. So, relationship after relationship or I guess I will call them relationships because I'm pretty sure that the men that were in them couldn't have considered them that, the most valuable thing that I thought I had to offer was between my legs.

And the funny part is that it doesn't matter how amazing what you have between your legs is, it should not and does not define or make you worthy, it doesn't make you enough but here I was placing all my value and all of my worth in this dark wet spot. So what do you think happens when it's not enough? They don't love you, they don't treat you right, they don't stay, now in the back of your mind is like oh damn I'm not even worth that, so what's left? Mind you at this point I have graduated college, I have master's degrees, I've accelerated my career professionally, started organizations headed up foundations and done a lot of things but none of that mattered because of all of these little breadcrumbs that were dropped, little seeds planted in my life growing up that have blossomed into these 60-foot evergreen trees blocking out all the sun, all the happiness, all the joy and all the amazing things that are trying to reach me but they can't get to me because these evergreen trees are blocking out all the sunshine so I get to live in a world of mediocre sunshine mostly dark and cloudy.

For most of my life, I guess you could say I was on the heavier side but as life went on I had to find other ways to hide and I guess for me food became a comfort. It was the only thing that never let me down, so I enjoyed it. But the physical weight on the outside had nothing to do with the weight of all the pain and all the trauma and everything I was carrying on the inside. It was just a physical manifestation of it. So, at 310 pounds if I didn't think men wanted me for anything more than sex before, I definitely didn't think they wanted anything more now. But if you knew me at that time you would've never thought that to be true. I had mastered walking around in this façade of happiness and joy and confidence that everyone around me bought into.

I had fooled myself so much that I was able to fool others. And then one day I realized that for me to lose weight on the scale I had to get rid of some of the weight in my soul. I had to forgive some people. I had to forgive myself. I had to get to know myself. I had to figure out who the heck I was underneath these 310 pounds because all this weight was everything that I was carried from 4 or 5 years old.

So, imagine if every hurtful thing that was said or every Traumatic experience was a pound and it was put in a bag so now you have to carry this bag every day, everywhere you go. I was. carrying these 310 pounds of hurt, pain, insecurities, uncertainties, questions, of doubt, everywhere I went. It gets tiring! I didn't know it then, but I've learned it now. Just like when you're in the gym and you lift weights, lifting this weight all the time builds muscle, builds. fortitude builds endurance. And the fact that I was able to carry all of that with me for so many years when I was finally able to put all that weight down the woman that was left standing there was stronger than anybody could imagine. The weight of the weight built my muscle.

Invisible Love

Fumbling through my thoughts with no clear direction.

Completely misunderstood by self.

Unsure of which thoughts are true but absolutely mesmerized with the idea.

Is there love or has it been dried up and left destitute like the terra incognita of Egypt?

Has it been abandoned or is the seed firmly planted beneath the dirt fortified with hope... waiting... for that isolated raindrop to inseminate its growth.

A reflectionless reflection of a mystery that too many have viewed but none have seen.

A painted picture all in white, so effortlessly wrapped in a golden frame.

A deep gasp for air amidst the water.

A Navy ribbon in the black sky.

A pre-conception of a misconception of a believable fallacy that is nothing more than truth.

I sit again, fumbling through my thoughts as if knowing my destination but having no clear direction.

Why have you consumed this space?

Did you not see the sign?

No vacancies... Max capacity reached but you... as disrespectful as a mannerless child have set up shop here.

Disregarding the necessary precautions and doing what you do so well... with your mischievous,

lackluster demeanor you have strolled your ass into my no-fly zone and fuck shit up.

You, you, you...

I sit here fumbling, through this invisibly visible, misconstrued understanding of a fallacy that is life.

Silence, deafening silence as thoughts of you consume my mind, manifesting into bone-numbing fear of a road so seemingly paved to a life only known to little girls who have yet to find out

that Barbie 's dream house doesn't exist and little boys whose imaginations perpetuate a misconstrued reality that they too can fly.

I fight myself as I begin to drift back into a place of disbelief.

Ignorantly blinded by a fictitious sense of happiness.

Momentarily slipping back into that moment when I too believe in white horses and knights in shining armor.

One brave enough to face the dragon that lives in me and reclaim that sweet smell of innocence that has long been destroyed.

But here you are, strolling into a space that has never been seen, the volt of uncharted land yet to be cultivated.

Planting seeds of nutrients and disturbing unsettled earth that has been the cracked foundation of this broke building.

Knocking down walls and laying plans to reinforce the faulty lines.

Completely ignoring the eviction notices and death threats you so nonchalantly continue to trespass in this war zone.

Sparked emotions flutter in my space, faint curls of a line typically straight.

Capturing time as if the sun's revolutions have been paused and set to stand still and beam light into a shadow that was cast long ago.

You are here. Uninvited, but yet making yourself at home.

No manners, completely unapologetic for intruding in a setting that was arranged to function smoothly.

Disrupting a system that had adapted to the task at hand, you have planted a virus and crashed this system.

This cold hard case is built to protect...

You with your sharp tongue and powerful words have taken god 's plan and put it on your back.

Through it, I cannot run, from it I cannot hide.

So, in this silence, I stand.

Deafening silence as thoughts of you consume my mind, manifesting into bone-numbing fear of a road seemingly so effortlessly paved...

So perfectly painted in what I foolishly thought was love.

Well Gems, as you can imagine, walking around with this false sense of self, insecurities, and confusion, doesn't exactly lend to a great foundation for love in your life. I've had three real loves in my life and it's still interesting to call them loves in my life because as much as I loved them and they claimed to have loved me when it came time to make a decision, I wasn't whom they chose. You might find it even more interesting to know that none of these three is my ex-husband. Shocking right? Don't get me wrong, I loved my ex-husband, and I cared about him but at that time in my life, I was in such a hurt space that I was determined never to love anyone the way I had loved before because I didn't want to be hurt, so there was a wall up now. But we'll talk more about that relationship in a few.

Throughout most of my life when it came to guys, I wasn't the pick of the litter. I wasn't the girl that most guys wanted, I didn't look the part. I didn't fit the bill. I had relationships here and there but many of them were me settling for what I thought were my only options.

It's really difficult to want to find genuine love when you don't know yourself, when you don't actually love yourself, and when everybody else is dictating you're worth for you and you've just conformed to what they've said. And in true fashion, this is exactly what happened to me. One of the 3, there's really not a whole lot to say there. We were high school sweethearts and he died early. It left a huge hole in my heart to lose someone, one of the only people who actually saw me. It was devastating. Even with how great our relationship was at such a young age, it didn't go without its shared trauma. There I was engaged to the man I loved, who has just been taken from me suddenly, having just lost our baby earlier that same year, to now only find out, while sitting at his funeral, that he had a 1-year-old son. Talk about a knife to the heart! I'm not sure which hurt more. Having this feeling of betrayal by him and then by God. I felt like God had betrayed me. Why take my baby and then take him? Why was her baby so special? It sent me into a serious spiral. To make matters worse, who was I going to talk to? Most people felt like he was too "handsome" for me anyway. So, after that, I kind of built this wall around my heart. I never wanted to feel that type of pain again. So, I told myself that I would only love but so much. I wouldn't allow myself to love someone as much as I loved him so that if anything happened, I wouldn't feel that type of devastation. But unfortunately, sometimes it's easier said than done with the two other individuals who found their way to break down the wall and make their way to the side.

These relationships came at two very different points in my life one starting in childhood and making several reappearances in high school, college, and young adulthood, and then the second one coming later in life, in my early 30s. But as far apart as they were they were almost the same exact relationship. And in retrospect, they both did the same amount of damage. Do you know what it's like to love someone with your entire heart, to be their best friend, even some would say soulmate? To be chosen in every aspect of their life except for the moment when they had to the real choice. Yeah, it really messes your mind up. Especially for someone who is already struggling with accepting or understanding their value and their worth. So, what does it say when someone can acknowledge you as their soulmate or is unable to pinpoint anything that you did wrong or anything that's wrong with you but for some reason when it came time to choose they chose somebody else? This has probably been one of the biggest questions that I've ever had to bear. If your soulmate didn't choose you then who will? I walked around with this question looming over my head for years. And one situation, having to accept the fact that it is what it is and it can never be and letting that go only to have that person come back years later and let me know that they feel like they made a mistake and to apologize for not valuing who I was back then when they had the chance. What the hell do I do with that information now?

Then to have the other situation be a constant mirror reflection of not being chosen. Being everything and all things except that one thing. Constantly watching someone choose others over and over but all the while making you their safe space. Who or where was my safe space? How narcissistic. But I allowed it. So, I could no longer blame them. I stayed, and I tolerated it, so I had to change.

Remember, my ex-husband, well that relationship was doomed from the start. A combination of the wall I had up, my insecurities, and my warped idea that my options were slim, I played it safe, or so I thought. There's a certain way you should love a person before making them your spouse and although I cared for him, it wasn't that type of love, but that's how I wanted it. My ex had things that I thought I could help him fix. If I could help him be and do better, then maybe he'd love me enough to treat me right. And despite how completely lopsided it was the "fat girl" had a man. But sadly, I had him and so did everyone else. I spent more money than I can count on bail, lawyers, his kids, his wardrobe, you name it, I took care of it. I made excuses for him, justified his horrible decisions, and did everything I could to try and "better" him. I probably should have used all that time and money to "better" myself. Although in my mind, I thought that by being married and doing what everyone expected of me at that age somehow the insecurities would disappear. But my marriage did the exact opposite. It made it worse. I gained so much weight and ended up in horrific debt and all those questions that existed before were now inflated. Here I was taking care of this man and he was cheating on me, talking about me with other women, belittling me, having more children and I could go on for a whole chapter.

My worth at this point was nonexistent so I stayed, for NINE years! Pretending, and fading more and more by the day. I faded so much that I tried to fade completely. What was the point of staying in this life?

Now I See Me

Fading in and out of consciousness, not fully sure of where I was, I could hear beeping sounds and voices. Was I dreaming? Was this heaven? What's going on?

"Ms. Vanderpool, Ms. Vanderpool" I could hear a voice say. "Welcome back". Still extremely groggy, I searched to find where the voice was coming from. Everything was a blur. As things began to focus, tears began to run down my face. Feeling the oxygen mask on my face and the IV in my arm, the voice became clearer and the person more visible.

"Glad to see you're still with us," a new voice said. Several hours before, I had consumed several sleeping pills and a bottle of wine in hopes of getting "some rest". I had managed to in a completely delirious state make my way to work that morning before I lost it. It was vaguely coming back to me. The tears began to fall again. Had I gotten so low that my value and worth had reached zero? Did I no longer want to be here?

"So, what are we going to do here?" I heard the voice say again. Was he talking to me? "Even though you didn't think so, clearly the man upstairs has a bigger plan for you," he said again "

So, what are we going to do?" he repeated. He went on to tell me how lucky I was to be alive because with what they pumped out of my stomach they have no idea how I made it through the night much less till the next day. Some of you may be thinking, why is the doctor talking to her like that? But sometimes you have to hear the hardest things at the hardest times in order for it to get through your hard head. I needed someone or something to snap me back. I had to come to some realizations. I had to come to the realization that the most important person that needed to choose me, was me because God already did. Understand, I'm not saying that it's that simple or easy and but with all of this from childhood to adulthood thinking that I wasn't enough and that something was missing, or I must look a certain way all the time, all I had to do was choose me.

The minute I learned to choose myself, no one else could define my worth or tell me whether or not what was between my legs constituted my value or if the scale says 150 pounds or 310 it doesn't make me any more or less valuable because I choose me.

Flaws and all, work in progress, I choose me. And every day, I make a conscious effort to choose myself. Suffering from depression is an everyday journey. It doesn't just go away. You must learn and identify your triggers. You must be aware of when your mood and thoughts shift. You must check your thoughts. You can't allow yourself to slip. You must know yourself.

Gems, if you don't take anything away from this chapter, please remember this:

The closest you've come to defeat is thinking you were going to be defeated!!! Sometimes it takes things falling apart for better things to fall into place. Sometimes it takes the most uncomfortable path to lead your life to the most beautiful place. You'll never see the purpose of the storm until you see the growth it produced. You'll never see the purpose of someone leaving your life until you see it was best for your life. You'll never understand why you went through what you went through until you see the strength, the power, and the resilience that it built inside of you.

Your current situation is not your final destination. Just because something is over doesn't mean your life is over. The pain that you're going through will soon turn into the pain that you conquered. That pain will become power. That weakness will become a strength. and that confusion will become peace. Better things are coming for your life. Every day is a new beginning.

Treat it that way. This chapter is your story. This moment is not your identity. This pain is not your life. The tables in your life will turn. Your heart will heal. Your tears will dry. It will take time, but things will get better. I know right now that's hard to believe when life seems unbearable, but this chapter in your life will come to an end. Seasons change.

Life is a marathon, not a sprint...and you are your biggest competition. Love yourself then work hard to be better than yourself. If you compete with yourself every day to be better than you were yesterday, you'd be surprised by what you can accomplish.

The people in your life either give you weight or wings. You decide. If you are not appreciated,

Don't be angry, that just means you are in the wrong place. Don't stay in a place where no one sees your value. Know your worth and know where you are valued. A diamond can't shine on the bottom of a cave.

Most importantly, know that God will make it what it is to be. Slowly but surely, he will guide you in what you need to do. He created you...every single part of you! And there is a purpose in you being here. Never let anyone define who you are. You are whom God says you are! So chose you. Love you. Be you. And Always...SEE You!

Back then, they saw me but I didn't. Now... I SEE Me and now They Don't!

Sincerely,
The MVPen

Soul Remission

Sam Moore

Still. Still your mind. Still your heart. Still your body. What you have just experienced is a spiritual operation. In order to properly heal, you need to be still for a moment. For moments. Sit in it. Sit with it. The shock that you are feeling is a correction consuming the spirit and piercing the soul. It feels heavy, some may say at times, it feels chaotic.

After the stillness comes conditioning, taking what has been corrected and building its strength through intentional exercise. There is still work to be done. Diligently, consistently and inevitably, painfully. All for the greater good. It is not enough to just have the operation, that is just the beginning. An operation is a method that is used to obtain a certain goal, but it is not the cure, it is the catalyst. There are times in life when you do not realize just how ill you are until you have the antidote.

Once you have the knowledge, what happens next? Deep work. What does deep work mean, really? The definition of deep work is the ability to concentrate deeply on a difficult task for prolonged periods of time without getting distracted. This means, emotionally, you are tasked to position yourself in an intentional space to unpack what you have discovered and learned. To isolate yourself and focus on your healing and the new places and spaces that will lead you. To be open to growing pains that ultimately lead to growth. To re-evaluate all areas of your life.

It is time to re-examine your worth and to put everyone on notice. It is time to choose yourself. Choosing yourself will not only affect your immediate life, but generations to come.

A Diamond is valued by four different areas, known as the "4 C's": Cut, Color, Clarity, and Carat.

Come on this journey with me as you assess and manage your value, but most importantly, give yourself permission. Permission to heal, to live, and to become.

Cut. A Diamond has three types of cuts: Shallow, Ideal, and Deep. Much like life, you have the opportunity and the decision to become as deep (or stay as shallow) as you decide to heal yourself. You are used to living cutting you down, in many ways, you've become accustomed to it. There are so many instances where others have done you wrong, but since we are being honest here, there are also many instances where YOU have been the one to cut your own self. It is time to sit in forgiveness, not just of others, but most importantly, of yourself. Forgive yourself for all of the times that you allowed yourself to compromise or be compromised for the sake of avoiding rejection, or the deep-rooted fear of not being enough. Forgive yourself for the instances where you said "yes", when your gut clearly told you to say "no". Forgive yourself for pouring into others so much, that you allowed yourself to remain empty. Forgive yourself for not going after that job, that dream, that move. Forgive yourself. For you my dear, are cut from a different cloth, therein lies the canvas of your value.

Color. It is rare to find a colorless Diamond, color is natural, and quite honestly, adds to the beauty and uniqueness of a Diamond. During our lifetime, our color has been challenged, and for some of us, it has been stripped from us. You have been told, time and time again, that the colorless version of you is the version that will help you attain success. To not be "so much" or to not do "too much". I am more than certain, your color, from your skin to your hair, your eyes, to the way you speak, walk, dream, and dance...the color of YOU is what will make you soar. Sometimes your color scares people, it makes them see the lack of luster in their own lives, so instead of focusing on their pain points, their response is to make you feel insecure and wrong about the very beauty and essence of you. Do not subscribe to that projection. Take your brush, and paint your life in any color you want. You are the artist.

Clarity. A Diamond's clarity is assessed by its total imperfections. Superficial imperfections are considered blemishes, while the deeper ones are considered inclusions. Just like our journey in life, you have had experiences that affected you deeper than others. Each experience creates the sum total of your outlook in life. Certain experiences and interactions shape the lens through which you look at your life, and how clearly you look at your life. There are things that happen in your life that are simply out of your control, but what is in your control is how you allow that to shape your view of life. Life comes with a myriad of ebbs and flows, ups and downs, highs and lows, some more devastating than others. The accountability you choose to take for your own life, and your outlook, molds and shapes the blessings that you chose to see. Sometimes choosing to see and acknowledge the smallest blessings can lead to the greatest ones of your life.

Carat. A popular misconception about a Diamond is that its worth lies within the size of the carat. The truth is, a Diamond's worth and how much it shines and sparkles lie within a meticulous cut. You could have a large carat that is worth much less than a smaller carat, simply because of the cut. Society makes us focus on quantity way more than quality, in every way. It is up to you to hold tight to your ideals and values, put an end to looking at the woman to your right or to your left, comparing your journey to hers. Shift that center of attention and look into the mirror. No matter how difficult it might be to reposition your focus on yourself, it is necessary. You cannot restore what you do not recognize. It is necessary to pour into yourself, to speak over yourself, and to be clear of your worth. Do not allow others to make you chase dreams and things that you have not been called for. Those are simply distractions. Get real with not only the type of life you want, but the life you DESERVE, then, confidently go for it.

As women, we wear multiple hats, sometimes all in one day. We put everyone else first as our name drops lower and lower on the care list. We relinquish control of our own lives for the sake of others. I am telling you now, choosing yourself is not selfish, putting yourself first is not selfish. You cannot pour from an empty vessel. Your spouse/significant other, children, family, friends, ministry, career, and purpose all suffer when you choose to always put them first and not actively and intentionally pour into yourself. Sometimes it is putting YOU first that shows your love for someone or something in a great manner.

This is your permission to take the time you need to sit in your healing and become a new creation. This is your permission to change to morph. This is your permission to put yourself first. This is your permission to press play. This is your permission to stop living tepidly, to live unabashed and loud.

It truly does not matter what you have done, where you have been, or where you have come from. You, my darling, are worth everything good in this world, it is up to you to believe it. The price of admission is that you do your part and heal.

Made in the USA
Columbia, SC
28 April 2023

15608707R00076